From the Sands
of
Iwo Jima

By William R. Henderson

Published by: **Higher Standard Publishers**
A division of Higher Standard Enterprises, Inc.
www.higherstandardpublishers.com

From the Sands of Iwo Jima
Copyright © 2007 by William R. Henderson

p. cm.
ISBN: 978-1-60402-532-3
Printed in the United States of America

1. Henderson, William R.

TABLE OF CONTENTS

Part II

Dedication

This book is dedicated to my Father and Mother, the Reverend Marion Charles and Ollie Maud Henderson, to whom I owe a debt I can never repay, and to my wife, Dorothy Saunders Henderson, who helped make me more than I am.

I want to express my deep appreciation and admiration to Julie McClennen who took my sorry collection of rambling notes and created a story, which I trust is worth your time and attention. Also, thanks to William, Selena, and Tiffany Owens of Higher Standard Publishers who took upon themselves the burden of publishing this book and for all the wise counsel which they generously shared with me.

Thanks to Scott Brown and his father, Bill Brown, for their persistent encouragement that provided the motivation to undertake recording my life experiences, and to Doug Phillips of Vision Forum for creating a visual record of my life defining experience during the Iwo Jima Campaign.

Time and distance has a way of fogging the memory and the events recounted in this book may not have necessarily occurred exactly as they are told but are reported as best as I remember them.

Part I

War Time

It is not the critic who counts, not the man who points out how the strong man stumbled or where the doer of deeds could have done better. The credit belongs to the man who is actually in the arena, whose face is marred by dust and sweat and blood; who strives valiantly; who errs and comes short again and again; who knows the great enthusiasms, the great devotions, and spends himself in a worthy cause; who at the best, knows in the end the triumph of high achievements; and who, at worst, if he fails at least fails while daring greatly, so that his place shall never be with those cold and timid souls who know neither victory nor defeat.

-Theodore Roosevelt

Chapter 1

March 2005, D-Day + 60 years

IN THE YEARS SINCE I'VE BEEN HERE, Iwo Jima has changed little. My first view of her is out the window of the plane. While I had seen aerial shots of Iwo when we were planning for Operation Detachment, I had never been overhead in the planes myself. We had studied the various perspectives, her topography laid out in two dimensions, pictures incapable of capturing the nature of the volcanic ash that made up the beaches or uncovering the system of caves that ran for 16 or so miles ingeniously concealed beneath the surface. None of that showed up in the aerial photographs, and none of it was visible now. Just the same stretches of what looked like innocuous black sand, hillocks dotting the interior, the priceless airstrips stretching fingers of white, and Mt. Suribachi looming in the distance.

The Japanese have protected the island as a shrine; the result – one of the most intact battle-grounds in history. Japan lost almost every one of the 22,000 soldiers who fought to hold on to Iwo Jima for as long as possible, and many of their remains still lay entombed in the cave systems, pill boxes, and spider holes that riddle the island. Our own dead were neatly laid to rest in a graveyard on the west side of the island. The island was both battleground and graveyard from end to end, and it served as a tangible example of my memories of the war - intact, untouched, and isolated.

Visiting in a contingent of about 200 Marines to celebrate the 60th anniversary of D-Day at Iwo Jima, I came on this trip with mixed emotions. I'm not sure about the other 60 or so Iwo Jima veterans that made the pilgrimage, but for me, Iwo Jima didn't haunt me as it may have many others. When I left Iwo Jima, left Japan at the end of the war, I closed that segment of my life. There was little to be gained by struggling with the memories of death and the price we paid for freedom during the 36 days I spent in close combat on Iwo Jima and the half year I spent cleaning up in Japan. Yet for others, for my family and friends, for Vision Forum Ministries who organized and were documenting the trip, my experiences serving in WWII remained a curiosity. My son, Chip, and my two grandsons, William and Nicholas, sat nearby, captivated by the view and by the sense of monumental history this small island represented.

Our plane circled Iwo Jima completely. I noticed very few visible signs of the tanks and amtracs left on the beaches. During the invasion, the beaches had been crowded with them, mired in the volcanic ash, left for dead. Those unable to be extracted were buried by years of surf crashing against the beach and shifting volcanic sands; those remnants of our attack were entombed in the sand that originally bogged them down.

We put down on an airstrip near Japan's weather station on Iwo. Our contingent appeared fairly solitary compared to the over 800 ships and boats in the original flotilla. These vessels comprised the attack force that debarked from numerous ports and rendezvoused in Saipan for the final leg of the trip. Being able to land on the island now as tourists stood in sharp contrast to our original purpose, that of securing Iwo Jima to stage flights capable of reaching the Japanese mainland, capable of stopping the men responsible for Pearl Harbor.

Pearl Harbor was the catalyst for many of us who had volunteered for service. Within days of the attack on December 7, 1941, thousands upon thousands of young men had reported to recruiting centers nationwide, feeling a call to duty, honor, and country when such a phrase wasn't yet a cliché. I remember that day - it was a Sunday morning, and

I had risen early to eat breakfast and attend church at Wesley Memorial United Methodist. After church, I was just finishing lunch with some friends from High Point College in High Point, North Carolina where I was a senior. There was an announcement that the Japanese had attacked Pearl Harbor. The air exploded with talk after the initial stunned silence. Reports of the war in Europe suddenly telescoped into our own backyard. On December 8, we gathered in the fraternity house to listen to President Roosevelt address the nation. I was outraged as I listened to the President describe what had transpired on the day he referred to as a "day of infamy." The room echoed with the committed voices of my fraternity brothers: "We have to join up!" and "We'll show them Japs not to mess with Americans." The following day we traveled to Raleigh, North Carolina, to volunteer in the Marine Corps.

I had grown up on a steady diet of allegiance, first to God, then to family and country. As a result, our collective decision to volunteer in the wake of the attack on Pearl Harbor was instinctive. None of us were so far removed from the realities of our migrant roots and the promises America held, from the memories and stories of World War I, or from the effects of the Great Depression that we would have thought twice about serving our country at such an hour. I had even considered, in the event the United States stayed out of the war, the possibility of crossing the border into Canada to join their military, which was already fighting overseas. For most of us, the debt we owed to our ancestors for our freedom and opportunities was still very tangible, even if our country's government had come late to that realization.

The ideas of duty, honor, and country were concepts that we lived daily, concepts that formed the backbone of who we were. As I stood on Iwo Jima again, I worried that these same concepts today are only evoked in extreme circumstances and rarely sustained long enough to see our nation through. Americans, it seemed to me, had grown content to live on the memories of great battles and outrages like Iwo Jima and Pearl Harbor. They would paint heroics in romantic terms and leave the actual ideals that carried the soldiers through those battles and experiences, the ideals that could unite a nation and keep one neighbor looking out for another, to others or perhaps to another time.

On this memorial visit, we scaled Mt. Suribachi in complete safety, my son and grandsons and I, along with the rest of the visitors. The volcanic ash, like hard kernel corn, slipped beneath our feet and made gaining forward momentum difficult. I pointed to where, sixty years ago, I had watched and relayed orders from the base of Mt. Suribachi with Colonel Johnson, while 1st Lieutenant George Schrier took a group of men and a flag to the top. I talked about the ingenuity of General Kuribayashi's plan for the defense of Iwo Jima and the strength and fortitude with which the Japanese soldiers fought. I told my grandsons how Kuribayashi instructed his soldiers to kill at least ten Americans before they died. I told them how the Japanese soldiers probably had even less hope of survival than we did, and frankly, we had precious little. I walked with my family over that island, paused to look at cave openings, marveled at pill boxes blown open, and played a game to see who could spot the craftily hidden spider holes. I shared with them what I could; I sensed they wanted more.

How could I explain to them the experience of Iwo Jima? It would be like trying to describe the taste of chocolate to someone who has never tasted it. They had read history books and seen movies. Perhaps they felt they were up to the task of filling in the blank spots with images and sounds, action borrowed from other scenes. My descriptions could be at best two dimensional, like the maps of Iwo Jima we had studied. How could I bring the war alive for them? How could I do it even though I didn't want to? While I dug for words, the images floated to my mind instead, images I had laid to rest years ago in their own graveyard. There are some things so unpleasant and tender that it hurts the soul to recall them. I did not want the memories scattered across my subconscious like the Marines' bodies were scattered across Iwo Jima. But most of all, I did not want my son and grandsons to see me as something that I wasn't – a hero. I had left all of them, all of the heroes, behind on Iwo Jima. I have yet to meet a Marine who fought there who felt differently.

Yet the stories serve their purpose. I thought of Colonel Liversedge tasking me on the ship back to our base camp in Hawaii with writing the official report of our battalion's part in the battle for Iwo Jima. I would write and write, combing my memories of days driven forward by adrenaline, by the desire to stay alive and be victorious, and by the desire not to disappoint the Marines, my family, and God. Colonel Liversedge would read a portion of the report and send it back to me: "More details, Henderson!" "More blood, Henderson!" It finally dawned on me some years later that Colonel Liversedge had provided me with a great honor in asking me to write that report, entrusting me with making sure history was accurately recorded.

At the end of the memorial visit to Iwo Jima, my son suggested that I write my memories down. At 82 years old, I was well aware that still having my memories was a luxury. I had already suffered a heart attack and a stroke; age was gaining momentum. But I had never been one to dwell on the past. Satchel Paige once said, "Don't look back; they might be gaining on you." I stuck with that philosophy. I had no pictures of my youth, only two pictures from my time in the service, and very few other mementos. For official reasons I had saved papers from my military and government service, but those remnants would provide my family with few answers as to who

I was and what had shaped me, which was in part what had shaped them.

One of the men on the trip gifted me with a small glass bottle of volcanic ash from Iwo Jima, "sand" from Green Beach. It was on this beach that I landed on February 19, 1945, and, by the grace of God, managed to survive when thousands of my comrades had died. Sitting at my desk with that small bottle of sand at the top of my blotter, I realized that I could give my family what they were asking for, my story of Iwo Jima, my story of business successes and failures, government posts taken and passed up, and my story of my faith and how certain values and beliefs carried me through life whether it took place on Iwo Jima, in a board room, or at home around the dinner table. I felt an overwhelming urge to confess, to be an apologist, a witness for a life viewed as extraordinary by some but that in reality ought to be a testament to the power of God to take a humble man and send him down a path. In my eighty-two years, I had lived through the Great Depression; I had seen men land on the moon; I had survived the costliest battle our nation has known; and I had made a fortune, lost it, and made another. I had watched the landscape of my life and the lives around me shift and change. Through it all, God's hand remains as visible at the end as it was at the beginning. As I looked at that small bottle of sand from Iwo Jima, I realized how desperately I wanted to share this with my family and others.

Chapter 2

An Ordinary Life

I GREW UP AN ORDINARY BOY IN NORTH Carolina on the eve of the Great Depression. That fact - of the Great Depression, not my birth - had little consequence for my family as my father was a Methodist preacher by the time I was ready to start school. That is to say, our economics were already greatly depressed. There was a saying that if the Lord would keep a Methodist preacher humble, the congregation would keep him poor. Both sides upheld their bargain in shaping my father and my family.

I cannot say what consequence my birth had, second son with an older brother named M.C. Several years later, a sister named Ruth followed. I was neither the first-born child of great expectations nor the baby of the family. I tagged along behind my older brother and spent as much time at my father's side as I could, a shadow to both.

The world into which I was born was much different than the one I live in now. When I say we had little but the Lord and each other keeping our family together, that is not an exaggeration. There was also little to divide us - no constant bombardment from television commercials or questionable music lyrics to threaten our moral health or take up valuable time. Christianity was the dominant religion in each of the small towns in which my father ministered. No Christian church competed on one corner with a synagogue on another, a mosque on a third, and a Buddhist temple on a fourth. We spent as much time as possible out of doors, pursuing our imaginations in play and supporting our family's finances with extra side work. Chores were a given, not a choice. And the Bible was as steady a part of our daily diet as food and water.

My father, M.C. Henderson, started out as an assistant manager of a retail store in Kannapolis, North Carolina. Shortly after I was born on September 17, 1922, my father felt called to Christian ministry. So we moved, the first of eight times, to Rutherford, NC, so that my father could attend Rutherford College, a small college sponsored by the Methodist Church in the western part of the state. The college made up the main social and business environment for the community, although there was a small textile manufacturing facility too. My early years were marked by the memory of my father going to school during the day and struggling over his homework in the evening. He was a good student, so perhaps struggling is not the best way to describe his academic pursuits; however, it is a good description of how he related to the study of Latin and Greek.

My father's studies and subsequent ministries set an example and a pace for our family life. I would venture to say that my father's hard work and expectations set the bar by which I measured every endeavor I undertook – that, and whether or not what I did was to the glory of God, an ideal which came from my father as well.

As an itinerant minister, my father's churches covered several small towns or villages. He would alternate between the towns' churches, visiting one on a Sunday, another the next Sunday. During the week days, he would make trips to the towns, meeting with the parishioners. Eighty years ago, the minister played an integral role in the town as communities were organized largely along religious and ethnic backgrounds. The people of these towns relied on the minister to guide them, with faith acting as the visible backbone of relations. Faith and the church were the glue that held these communities together.

In our family, faith was everywhere, but I would say my mother was the glue that kept us together – clean, well-fed, well-mannered (as possible), and respectful. She was my Sweetpea, the name I gave her as a child and what I called her until she died.

Her real name was Ollie Maud Henderson, and she was as proper a southern lady as one could hope to find. When my father decided to enter the ministry, she gave her full support and exemplified the "love your neighbor" aspect of the Scriptures on a daily basis.

"Into bed, Billy. You too, M.C. Get settled and we'll read for a moment or two," Sweetpea would say, tucking us in with the Bible pinned between her arm and side. "Who do you want to hear about tonight? David and Goliath? Shadrach, Meshach, and Abednego?" She brushed the hair from my eyes with the same hand she had smacked my fingers with earlier as I reached for the batter bowl. I grinned at her with the memory.

She was such a warm and comforting presence, even though she could be strict and harsh when needed. It was no easy task during the Great Depression to feed a family, let alone feed a family on a minister's wages. She stretched our money out, like a pie crust with barely enough flour, and then sweetened it with a smile.

My mother filled up the spaces in our lives created by a father who had to tend a flock spread across several different towns. He was like the modern day mail service – come rain or sleet or sunshine, there was a job to do and people who depended on him. We watched him leave one morning, through what seemed like two feet of snow with more coming. He opened the front door and let in a blast of icy coldness, so cold that his breath froze before he crossed the threshold. With his back straight and his body bundled to my mother's specifications, he set out for the seven mile walk because he had a job to do and he knew the folk in this area wouldn't let weather stand in the way of making it to church. Sure enough, when he came home, his feet nearly frozen stiff, he told us that over half the congregation had greeted him at the church.

Out of the three of us children, I followed my father the most, volunteering to walk or ride with him to the different churches and towns. I felt through my father and because of him an affinity for God that made me want for more. One night at a revival, which happened often in those times, I came and knelt before my father to receive Jesus as my personal Savior. I was six and a half. I was moved by the fervor and belief in my father's voice as he preached about the love of God and the salvation through His Son. I wanted it as much as I had wanted anything. I knelt before my father and felt his hand on my head before he moved on to the next person. Later he smiled at me, and for a moment it was just the two of us with the sweetest secret in the world.

When my father was home, he worked around the house, tended the garden, and went about the business of caring for the myriad of animals we kept to raise money. He loved his gardens. There was never a chore or pleasure that couldn't be turned into a lesson about character or faith. One evening, after I had spent a good bit of the afternoon weeding the garden, my father came to me and asked me to follow him outside.

"You see that bit of weeds there, Billy?" he asked.

"Yes, Dad," I said.

"When you do your work, Billy, you do your best. That's all I can ask. That's all God can ask. Not your best to be compared to what someone else can do, but your best. If you do your best, then you can rest." He left me then to finish. I got down on my knees and pulled those last few weeds I had overlooked or ignored. I was hot and sticky, looking forward to some lemonade and maybe a few minutes just watching the sun disappear. I didn't feel resentful. I felt sad at the tone of my father's voice; I didn't like hearing him have to talk to me that way. Oh, he never yelled. He was as pleasant a man as the road was long, but I felt what he said deeply.

Most of our activities revolved around the church and the school. Despite the general lack of money, or maybe more so because of it, we grew up finding pleasure in the simplest of things. Snow cream was one of them. Few stores carried ice cream in the winter, so a bountiful snow was an event we celebrated by mixing fresh snow with flavored milk to make snow cream. I remember one particular winter when we awoke to several feet of snow. I remember it because my sister arrived shortly after that snow, a tiny bawling bundle. As my father set out to make sure there had been no damage to the church, we stayed home making snow cream and eating it until we could eat no more.

The meager finances of the communities during the Great Depression brought the people together in shared work and play in ways I have not seen since. The idea that God can turn all things to good for those who trust in Him played itself out over those years and stayed with me. Neighbors shared the load - whether it was helping with labor, taking food to the less fortunate, or simply sharing company. I grew up watching God use unfortunate circumstances to bring out the best in people. We held corn-husking festivals, where families gathered at a farm to harvest and shuck corn, then play games and eat. We set out on foot together to take food to neighbors hit hard by the loss of savings or jobs – the expressions of thankfulness on their faces was always repayment enough. The lessons I learned in those growing years have remained with me, and I have never found myself wishing our finances had been otherwise so that we could have avoided our own hardships or helping others.

As for me specifically, I was a typical boy, not particularly athletic or intelligent. I grew into a tall and gangly boy, who spent many evenings playing war, building forts, and playing grown-up. Our finances were such that we, as well as most kids around us, spent a good deal of time coming up with ways to make extra money, which set me on the path of entrepreneurship early on. I was a child dedicated to being the servant given the five talents and turning them into ten. The Bible stated that "To those who use well what they are given, even more will be given, and they will have an abundance." I never held the delusion that I had much talent or brains, but I would use everything I had been given for as long as I had it.

Back then we grew, picked, raised, and sold anything and everything, with mixed success and mixed lessons learned. M.C. and I grew and sold beans in our modest garden. One year we raised calves to sell, but I came out on the losing end of that endeavor. Our house sat on a large grassy lot next to the railroad, and we would tether our calves there to graze. About halfway through the calves' young lives, M.C. found his had gone missing and wandered on to the train tracks.

"Billy, look how much the railroad company paid me," he said a few days later, showing me the $7.50 he earned for his calf foolishly finding its way in front of a moving train. If he earned $7.50 for a dead, useless calf half the size mine would reach before I sold it, I had high hopes for the price mine might bring in later.

"How much did you make?" M.C. asked me when I had finally sold my calf.

I showed him the $6.00 I had made, and we both did the mental math of subtracting out what I had paid in feed. I looked up at M.C. "Comes to about $4.00 for all the work. A half-grown dead calf for

$7.50 sure seems like the better end of it, doesn't it?"

I have no doubt that neither of us felt for the dead calf what we felt for the loss of money and time invested. This was even more apparent when we lost 200 or more chicks to an overzealous oil heater. With a loaned incubator, M.C. and I set about hatching a heck of a lot of chicks. We had a nice little chicken house, but we worried because the nights early in the season were cool, and the chicks were delicate and subject to getting cold and dying of shock.

"Let's put the portable oil heater in there and warm 'em up nice," M.C. said. (Frankly, I'm not sure if it was my idea or M.C.'s, but I'll let him take the blame.)

One weekend a few weeks after we had installed the heater, we returned home from our grandparents' home in Concord, NC, an hour or so away. We had lit the heater earlier, knowing we might be back late. We returned to a smoldering ruin of a chicken house and every chicken dead. That was a right mess to have to clean up. I could have cried if I were the crying type because those chickens had been at the two and a half to three pound size, a week away from market.

M.C. and I switched then to what we could raise in the garden. The idea of losing a dollar or more per chicken when the chicken house burned down had soured us on raising any more animals. We settled on butter, or lima, beans, which brought in 30 cents for a shelled quart. That was a lot of money for not too much work. Because we had to take our pay in trade, my savings didn't grow much, but I had all the ice cream and candy I could eat unless my mom needed something. That worked out okay for me that summer.

Of all the jobs I had as a youth, the one that impressed me the most was picking cotton. The impression I walked away with was that cotton-picking was not the job for me. With my overalls on, I would start early in the morning, before the heat made the air shimmer in waves. I had put my mason jar of water covered with cloth at the end of a row, like a big, shiny trophy waiting for me at the finish of a hard-won race. Then I would work my way down. The longer the day, the heavier the bag slung over my shoulder got until it was all I could do to drag it, and myself, from one cotton plant to the next. I left a trail of bright red specks of blood on the cotton I picked. The bole opens up into six or eight pedal-like growths with a needle like spur at the apex. I had to pull the cotton out of the bole; more often than not poking my hand on the spur before I could pry loose the prize. I was flinching in my mind before I had even gotten a firm hold on the cotton each time I reached to pick it. I wasn't afraid of hard work, but I decided after that summer of picking cotton that any hard work I did for life sure wouldn't be that job ever again.Farming, in general, was a hard, mostly thankless job. For several weeks out of the summer we would work on our grandparents' dairy farm. My grandfather Rufus, whose name was my middle name, had quit as superintendent of a textile mill of twenty years and arrived home to tell his wife, "I've quit my job and bought a farm. Let's pack up." We would work hard in the fields from sun-up to 4 o'clock. Not even swimming in the creeks or cold juicy watermelon after those hard, humid days could convince me that any kind of farming lay in my future.

The one job I truly enjoyed was working in a men's clothing store in Asheboro, North Carolina. About the time I reached 14, still too young to be officially employed, a friend of my father's, Osburn Yates agreed to let me work for free in his department store and learn something about retail. The first day I worked, God must have been smiling down on me. The economy was still depressed, and the men's clothing sales were rather slow. However, I managed to sell two men's suits and several other key pieces of clothing that day. Even though I had agreed to work for free, the Assistant Manager offered to pay me 50 cents each Saturday that I worked over the next several weeks. I did well enough that I soon was earning a commission. I found I had an interest in and a knack for selling men's clothing. I learned a great deal working for Mr. Yates, not just about retail though. He was a very courtly gentleman, intelligent and wise, and had earned the respect of not just his employees but the community as well. I saw in him an early glimpse of the kind of man I wanted to be, a bit like Mr. Yates and a bit like my father.

The list of my efforts to make money was fairly endless. I sold books about a nationally known flood that had occurred in Johnstown, Pennsylvania in 1935, literally pedaling them from the back of my bike from one community to the other. I had contacted the publisher and negotiated a price. I did the same selling Bibles, making $114 the summer of 1936. I thought I had found my pot of gold. However, considering the number of hours I worked, I probably wasn't making minimum wage. It kept me out of trouble, though and to a teenage kid, it was a fortune in 1936.

As far as athletics went, I had all the desire, but little of the natural talent. Football was the big sport when I was in high school, and playing sports was a big deal for boys. I had played basketball with some degree of talent because I was tall and wiry, but I really wanted to play football.

"Billy," the coach said, "why don't you be the team manager?"

I wasn't listening to the subtle suggestion behind the comment - I did not have the talent for football.

"No, Coach. I want to play football," I told him with all of my confidence and desire, as if those alone would hold me up against the boys on the other side of the scrimmage line. Unfortunately, there are some things that no matter how much you want them to be true or a part of your reality, they just aren't going to be. That was what I learned from that first day of football.

Coach lined me up opposite the players who were practicing blocking, and those guys nearly killed me.

"Coach," I told him after practice, "you've got yourself a team manager." Sometimes I was a slow learner. Not that day.

Towards the end of high school, one of the high school counselors pulled me aside to talk about the next step in my education. I had always paid much more attention to extra-curricular activities than academics since I had started school, never having fancied myself to be all that bright.

"Billy, I've got some exciting news for you," she said, bubbling over with excitement. I didn't know quite what to make of her at that moment. "Several colleges and universities have sent scholarship offers for you."

Looking back, I can only imagine my expression. Did she mean me? Scholarships for me?

"What am I getting scholarships for?" I asked.

"Do you remember the achievement tests you took last fall?"

"Who could forget the achievement tests we had to take last fall?" was what I wanted to ask. But I just said, "Yes, Ma'am."

"You scored well enough on them to earn the scholarships." She didn't tell me what my scores were and I didn't think to ask, still believing there had been some gross error. I remembered moving from one school district having completed fourth grade only to be placed in sixth grade in the new district based on testing. That was why I graduated a year earlier than normal. But that hadn't changed my estimation of my abilities. I suppose my unwillingness to believe my intelligence was anything above ordinary has kept me humble and hard-working in the long run.

I walked away from my parents' home and moved to college with as firm a foundation as to who I was as I could have hoped for. I had no delusions about being special, except in my parents' eyes and God's. I had learned the value of hard work, how and when to best use my talents, and what those talents were. I knew that a family and a community could survive any disaster by pulling together. And I knew that when my father drove me to High Point College and handed me $2 when he dropped me off, that he was placing not only a considerable amount of money in my hands relative to our family's finances, but that he was showing me a vote of confidence as to the man I had become.

"For I know the plans I have for you," declares the LORD, "plans to prosper you and not to harm you, plans to give you hope and a future. Then you will call upon me and come and pray to me, and I will listen to you. You will seek me find me when you seek me with all your heart."   *Jer 29:11-13*

Chapter 3

The Road to Iwo Jima

I HADN'T INFORMED MY PARENTS WHEN I volunteered for the Marine Corps in December 1941. My brother was already in the service stationed in Texas, though I don't know that that had anything to do with my hesitation to tell them. It wasn't until after I took and passed the physical, which several of my fraternity brothers failed to pass, that I called my parents and let them know the news.

My father was not surprised, but neither was he overjoyed. "Billy, if this is what you feel like you need to do, then you have to do it. I know you'll do fine," he told me on the day I called.

My father never seemed to have any doubt that I would acquit myself well in life, a fact that spurred me on in the most unlikely of circumstances and accounted for my reputation as the kind of man who worked hard and accomplished most of what he set out to do (football, or course, being an obvious exception). I never wanted my father to believe his confidence in me had been misplaced. A friend once told me he was talking to my father and asked him how I was doing in college. My father replied, "I'm not sure exactly what he's doing, but I'm sure he's doing all right. I don't have any concern that he'll not be all right." When my friend told me about this conversation, I filed it away and pulled it out like a worn photo any time I was tempted with the opportunity to do something that I desired but knew was not the right thing to do, or was challenged by some physical, mental, or emotional situation. I summoned up the courage to resist because I did not want to picture my father's disappointment.

My mother's reaction to my volunteering was colored by the fact that she already had one son in uniform and the realization that the war was no longer a problem for the soldiers of some other country. Pride because of our willingness to serve gave way in the face of her concern for our safety. While neither of my parents were overly demonstrative with their affection for us, I could hear the emotion in my mother's voice, the resignation and the fear, the understanding even so. We made small talk, circling around the obvious. She could have had no way of knowing what lay ahead for me at Iwo Jima, but general news of the war was enough to frighten any parent, even with the unshakable faith my parents shared.

My father's opinion of me carried me through basic training, and the quiet example of Christian manhood he exemplified throughout my youth. A person can know the shock of Marine Corps basic training in an intellectual way – the sergeants will yell and scream, they'll break the recruit down, and the urge to beg for relief from the physical demands or to quit will be overwhelming – I had known all that in my head, but it could not compare to the rude reality that starts before a recruit even drops his bag on the first day he reports for training.

In May, Parris Island was hot and humid already. I quickly discarded my clothes and donned the ever-present field of green from the skivvies I wore on the inside to my socks and hat on the outside. I replaced my affable nature when confronted by the training sergeant with the scowl necessary for the serious task ahead. And the sergeants and officers quickly notified each of us that whatever ideas we had about how special we were individually (I had few enough of those to begin with), that we were nothing but what we could be together. And so the yelling ensued, for weeks on end. "I'm not here to help you find yourself. You are who I tell you you are – a United States Marine. I don't care what food you like and don't like, what you do when you get up in the morning, or what order you like to read through the paper. You'll do *what* I tell you to do, *how* I tell you to do it, and *when* I tell you to do it. Look to your left and your right. By the end of this training you won't be able to tell yourself apart from the Marine on either side of you, which is good because when you save him, you'll be saving yourself."

The men in Smokey Bear hats did their best over the next four months to break us down; they sought to transform us with the vengeance of the devil himself. We dressed alike, we slept together, ate together, got up at 4:30 a.m. and ran several miles together, came back and showered together, cleaned latrines together, did KP together, and marched and drilled together, then marched and drilled together some more, and marched and drilled together some more. If any one of us showed a trait of individuality, the drill sergeant, in a fit of apoplexy, would give an order for the platoon to do push-ups or some other form of physical exertion meant to rid us of any vestiges of ourselves. We jettisoned our personalities like jetsam from a ship sinking fast. Our survival depended on lightening the load, until we resembled nothing more than the hulk of the ship with our sergeant controlling the sails.

In the end, it worked. We learned to pull together and help one recruit with shoe shining, another with fitness, and another with cleaning his rifle. A spirit of cooperation built within us. With unwavering discipline, numbing physical exhaustion, and repeated routine, something began to happen to us, guys from the Bronx, the Ivy League dandies, and the farm boys from Alabama. Slowly and imperceptibly, bonds began to form, not between individuals only, but bonds where one's identity was unit-oriented. We began to live what we had signed up for-to relate to something greater than ourselves, something worthy of pride, extracted in shared sacrifice and a feeling of community, loyalty, duty and honor to others who had endured the same ordeal. When historians write of the men who fought at Iwo Jima saying that uncommon valor was commonplace, those writers are talking ultimately about bonds and commitments that were practiced first on the brutal battlefield that basic training represented.

Working with people from different segments of society or different races was not foreign to me, a fact that made basic training from that perspective easier. In 1939, my last summer before college, my father secured a job for me through a friend, Mr. Everett Jordan, who later became North Carolina Junior Senator in Washington, DC. I was the only white young man on an all black crew installing sewers to the mill village houses, which were owned by the company. At that time in the South, it would have been unacceptable for me to work under a black supervisor, so Mr. Jordan, the owner of the mills, designated me as superintendent of the work crew. I knew I could only be superintendent in name only because I had little idea how to manage these men. The real superintendent was a large black man called

Big Sam. I deferred everything to Big Sam because he knew how to do the job much better than I did, and, more importantly, the crew respected him. There was no doubt in anyone's mind who was really in charge.

Big Sam was a very intelligent and gentle man with integrity. What he lacked in worldly possessions, he made up for in knowing exactly who he was and being secure in that. I watched him move and command the men, and I could only think of royalty. There was just something about his bearing and demeanor; the other men felt it too because they responded positively every time, no matter what Big Sam requested.

I have always been grateful for what I learned from Big Sam that summer. A man was a man was a man. In basic training it was no different – in my mind what mattered was whether as a Marine the fellow would do the job when the time came because my life might depend on it. A man's financial situation was not the currency that would ensure our survival in battle; the currency of basic training, and ultimately Iwo Jima, was strength, endurance, cooperation, faith, and hope. Well, sometimes the currency was extra K-rations or a good shower, but that only sustained a soldier for so long.

Some people manage to stay cocooned during their youth with the belief that wealth makes one superior, that poverty is simply a choice, and that ethnicity or skin color determines one's worth. At

Parris Island, I listened to the different accents in the low whispers at night and was thankful for being poor enough as a child that it wasn't a struggle to accept the men beside me, thankful that I knew that need came in a variety of packages, and that loss in its various forms came to everyone regardless of their standing in the community. What counted here was not the inflections of the voice or the weight of the pocketbook, but how hard a Marine was willing to work, how far a Marine was willing to push himself, and how willing the Marine was to sacrifice for the men to his right and left. I realized that Jesus Himself demanded no less from our everyday life as well.

The possibility of personal sacrifice and death were ever-present, even though we were only in training. War abroad and the surprise deaths during the attack on Pearl Harbor had brought most of us to Parris Island; the drill sergeants responsible for training us to think like Marines reminded us at every turn that our lives depended on each other; and the training deaths that occurred left us with no doubt that death was a probability because at Parris Island the training exercises were controlled, unlike the battlefield where anything could happen.

I remember completing one night mission during basic training when we were up to our chests in water with our packs on our backs. We held our rifles over our heads, moving forward slowly, cautiously, methodically. It was hard to tell what was going on beyond the men right around me. When the training exercise finished, we found out that one of our guys hadn't made it through the water. For the first time, the fact that I might not make it through even the training alive became a reality. I prayed for the young man's family, and then, truthfully, I prayed for my own safety.

We joked when we could, found little things to keep us going. My parents wrote me letters once or twice every ten days or so, pages filled with news of home, the necessities of daily existence that reminded me life was still taking place at a normal pace and in a normal way beyond the confines of Parris Island. Somebody out there still worried about whether the neighbor's daughter would ever get married and how the shopkeeper in town drank too much on a Friday night. Trips to the PX (post exchange) did much to lift our spirits and connect us to the outside world as well. Pogie bait, what we called candy, was an unexpected treat that turned the hardened, battle-ready grown men we believed ourselves to be into the children that still lurked behind the facade. Those small sweet pleasures allowed us momentarily to forget we were all about the business of learning to kill.

In many ways we were in the war already despite the fact that we hadn't left the States. The camaraderie kept us alive, physically and emotionally. Seeing past any differences among the men made relying on them and sacrificing for them that much easier.

The end of basic training brought relief, uncertainty, and no small amount of pride. Each recruit experienced the rigors of basic training differently – maybe for one it was the physical challenge that was nearly insurmountable, or living in close quarters with strange men, or processing the information that came at one as if from a fire hydrant - fast, steady, and voluminous. I had been worried to some extent about the physical aspect of training, but I was used to putting in more effort in order to make up for only an average amount of natural athletic ability. Many of my fraternity brothers who were more physically adept had not passed the initial physical exam. At Parris Island, the physical demands never stopped.

Despite my concerns, I was recommended to be a drill instructor at Parris Island once basic training was finished. I would receive my own Smokey Bear hat and a license to yell. From this side of the training, the contrast between the individuals who arrived for basic training and the unit that left at the end was so marked it was startling. They seemed so young. I had watched the men return to the same two-story wooden barracks at night to undergo what seemed like a magical daily transformation that turned these boys into men and men into one unit. It was an inspiring thing to watch.

Chapter 4

Training and Waiting

THE MARINE CORPS TOOK A BIT OF TIME to straighten out the paperwork that had relegated us college graduates to the enlisted ranks instead of the Officers' Candidate School slots we had been promised when we signed up. I saw it as a short course entitled "Welcome to the Military." Shortly thereafter, I received notification that I was cleared to go to Officer Candidate School at Quantico, Virginia. While Parris Island had been tough, particularly physically, Quantico was even tougher because it challenged us not only physically, but mentally and emotionally as well. Also, because the Marine Corps had been inundated with volunteers, they had an excess of junior officers. The mission of our time at OCS became not just about training but about pushing us to the point that sixty to seventy percent of the candidates in each class dropped out.

More than anything else, my father's words sustained me through the training at Quantico. I remembered those lessons in the garden as a child, when I was sent back out in near darkness to pick the weeds I had missed. "Billy," my father would say, "do your best and then you can rest." I would listen to other children about the business of playing while I grew sweaty in the heat that pressed around me despite the late hour. That lesson didn't have to happen more than once or twice before I realized doing a job twice wasn't worth it. So with every obstacle at Quantico, I did my best, even when someone else was faster or smarter, and in the end I found I always had a little bit more I could give even when I thought I was all used up.

My father's words and expectations tied closely to Bible verses I had memorized over the years came first in their ability to keep me moving forward and digging deeper. But when it came to lifting one's spirits, there was nothing like weekend liberty. We would go to New York and Washington and seek out female companionship at the USO. The music blared and the women's skirts swirled in time. They were all beautifully turned out, the women with their gloved hands, red-painted lips, and seamed stockings. I was thirteen or so when girls magically transformed like caterpillars to butterflies, from being annoying and beneath me to worth my interest. It was a game of hide and seek in the cornfields that did me in.

The memories of that night collided in a montage of images that all ended in a kiss. It was a warm autumn, and neighbors from all around had gathered for a corn-shucking party. I remember food and games, music and dancing. Out of that blur, a girl grabbed me during a game of hide-and-seek, and my neatly ordered world tilted with my first kiss. That was a new and exciting sensation. After that, I started to see girls everywhere and found I enjoyed their company even though I didn't understand them.

As I watched the women at the USO dance, I kept my father's treatment of my mother as a guide when it came to how to treat women. When we picked up women at the USO or in some of the nicer bars, we had a great time, though sometimes it required a lot of discipline to keep from going further. This attitude kept me from any serious entanglements. In all, our weekends were sometimes more challenging than our weekday training. No matter how hard we lived on Saturday night, I always tried to find a church Sunday morning, attending much of the time by myself.

When training at Quantico ended, I was commissioned a Second Lieutenant in the Marine Corps. We stood around comparing our assignments. I called out to my buddy, "Someone must have stepped on my IBM card with their golf shoe and punched the hole accidentally. They're sending me to chemical warfare and demolition school." We had a good laugh over shaky, old Bill designing and demolishing mines and bombs at Edgewood Arsenal in Maryland.

With the other trainees, I shed tears as we experienced the effects of the use of toxic gases. I blew up my share of objects in Maryland before I boarded a train bound for Camp Pendleton, California, one stepping-stone closer to the war in the Pacific. We talked, smoked, and played cards across the interior of the United States, rolling through one station after another with only vague ideas of what awaited us at the other end. I checked into Camp Pendleton in southern California, located between Los Angeles and San Diego, where a new division, the 5th, was being formed. Camp Pendleton had only been acquired in March, 1942, to be used as a tactical training area for the large Marine units that would be needed for the island campaigns in the Pacific. With 17 _ miles of beachfront and covering 130,000 acres at the time of purchase, Camp Pendleton served the same purposes on the west coast as the Camp Lejeune, NC, facility did on the east coast: a training operations facility for amphibious, ground, air, and support services. The 9th Marine Regiment marched from Camp Elliot in San Diego to Camp Pendleton to be the first unit to occupy the base. The 3rd Marine Division under General Lemuel Shepherd was the first major Marine unit to train at Camp

Pendleton, and my unit, the newly formed 5th Marine Division, would be the second.

When I reported to the 28th Marine Regiment, 5th Marine Division, there were only two officers in my regiment, a quartermaster major, and an adjutant with the rank of captain. I reported to the quartermaster major.

"Second Lieutenant William Henderson reporting, sir," I barked out, standing ramrod straight, my salute crisp.

"At ease, Lieutenant. Welcome to Camp Pendleton. I've got your first duty all lined up for you. We're a little tight on space, what with all the troops coming in. The permanent barracks are all full. You get the privilege of building the tent camp. It'll be great experience."

"How big, sir?" I asked. "How many men?"

"About 3,300," he replied. I waited for some indication that he was joking with me. It didn't come.

When I enlisted, I had indicated my interest in a military career, and here I was being assigned the task of building a tent camp for 3,300 men. I knew nothing about construction. As my desire to become a regular officer, or rather, my expressed desire for a military career, I was the likely candidate for any extra duties. My commanding officer, Colonel Liversedge, would say, "Well Henderson, when you're a regular officer, you will need this experience." I managed to gain all sorts of experience before I left

Camp Pendleton. As for the tent camp, it was fortunate for me that the Navy had an outfit called the Seabees, which was the construction unit for the armed forces. I quickly learned from them how things were done in the military.

I was a little bit miffed about having to live in a tent camp since over half of our regiment had already been in combat. Other regiments, most of whom hadn't seen combat, were housed in barracks. So we really did it up brown, which is to say we built the best tent camp the military had ever seen. We not only had an Officers' Club, but a club for all the non-commissioned officers in each of the battalions. We had air-conditioned mess halls because the Seabees C.O., Warrant Officer Garvey, was a genius. He set up a series of fans and had a cooling apparatus that cooled the water. By spraying it in front of the fans, it would chill the air. We were the only outfit in the Marine Corps who had air-conditioned mess halls. Unfortunately, we didn't have the tent camp hard-wired for electricity.

Securing electricity taught me two other major lessons: find the person with the connections and be prepared to take all the blame if anything goes wrong. I knew there was a major power line about a mile and a half away, so I went to see the old man, Colonel Liversedge. I asked him, "Sir, there's power about a mile up the road, and I wonder if we could get permission to tap into it?" The Colonel let me know he would look into it.

While Colonel Liversedge looked into it, I went about the business of training with the troops assigned to 28th Regiment. As officers, we had a duty to be up before our troops, to not go to bed until after them, and to eat after they had eaten. We set the example and the standard. I would not ask the enlisted men to do anything I couldn't do or hadn't already done. That way, when it came to fighting in battle, the enlisted men knew the officers leading them could be trusted and followed, a key component to surviving combat. So I would get up early in the morning and go out into the field before the other troops were up and did not get back to regimental headquarters until everyone was secure for the day. We trained for amphibious landings, ground assaults, weapons firing - anything and everything despite the fact that our exact mission was not yet made known to us.

When I came back to Headquarters early one day, someone said, "Are you Lt. Henderson? Please, Lieutenant, I have some mail for you." I said I would come over to pick it up, but he replied, "No, Sir, you can't carry it because there are two sea bags of mail." A sea bag is approximately 18 inches square and stands about 3 feet high. When I picked up the mail, I remembered a man we had met on the train to Camp Pendleton. A few of us had talked well into the night with this man who owned a chain of radio stations in the Midwest. Apparently, he broadcast about these Marines he met who were on the way to

Camp Pendleton. He talked about how lonely they were going to be and how nice it would be to send them a letter. Judging by how packed the sea bags were with mail, I imagined everyone in the Midwest must have written to us.

My bumper crop of mail came from women, girls, boys, and men, and contained everything from candy, to shaving lotion, pictures and even offers of marriage. I said, "Just throw the sea bags in my jeep," and I acted like it was normal for me to receive this much mail. The enlisted guys thought I was some big shot, and I never told them any different. Warrant Officer Garvey and I would read them. Some of them were really interesting and encouraging; some were just good for a laugh, which was what we needed. The country's support, so evident in the letters themselves and the sheer volume of them, comforted us in ways we couldn't have put in words. There were a lot of uncertainties ahead of us, though we were convinced death was likely, so the kind letters went a long way towards filling the gap between what we knew and what we could express out loud.

It wasn't long after the fan mail arrived that Colonel Liversedge informed me we were turned down on our request to bring electricity to the camp. I went to Warrant Officer Garvey, who had already proven on several occasions that he knew how to make things happen. I complained to W.O. Garvey about the situation – I felt justified in complaining because I was doing so on behalf of 3,300 men, not just myself. I kept thinking of my father who never complained the entire time he was alive. We once drove to my grandparents' home in the Concord, NC, area. We traveled in a Model T Ford from Democrat, NC, about 200 miles or so. The trip was punctuated by 13 flat tires, but my father's good cheer never wavered. He cheerfully pulled over, jacked up the car, repaired the flat, let the car down, and resumed driving, whistling all the while. I decided it was not time for my father's cheerful patience yet. There might still be some magic Warrant Officer Garvey could do.

"Lieutenant," said Garvey. When he said it, the word sounded more like "Looo-tenant" because he was from Louisiana. "Lieutenant," he said, "I know where there's enough wire to wire the whole camp. Get me some whiskey, and I can get the wire."

Since I was in charge of setting up the Officers' Club and could buy the booze very cheap, I secured him enough whiskey to grease the wheels with the people at the Naval warehouse in San Diego. Garvey managed to commandeer enough wire for the whole camp. When it came time to turn the camp over for final inspection, the commanding officer of Camp Pendleton walked through, followed by General Rocky who was the commanding officer of the 5th Division, then other dignitaries, and finally Colonel Liversedge. I was walking along behind Colonel Liversedge, as was the custom of the junior officer. They were admiring the work. The Seabees had really done a great job, they all murmured. Suddenly Liversedge stopped and waited for me to come alongside.

"Lieutenant," he said, "I don't remember getting approval to wire this camp. This whole camp is wired."

"Yes, Sir," I said.

"Did you wire this camp without approval?" he asked.

"Yes, Sir," I said.

He paused a moment and said, "I will never say a word about it, but if you get caught, it is going to be your butt" (except he used more graphic language). I shared this with Warrant Officer Garvey. Our only option was to wait and see whether there would be any fallout.

Training was rigorous. News trickled in via the wire, newspapers, and higher ups regarding the toll various battles were taking on our troops: ground we gained, ground we lost. We escaped every week-end we could on liberty in Los Angeles. I remember one friend asking me to double date with him be-cause his girlfriend would not go out with him unless he got a date for her friend. In an effort to convince me to go on a blind date, he told me that his girl's friend was a model. She was a model all right - she modeled fingernail polish. However, she was pleas-ant, and I enjoyed the evening. That was how I passed the time, with pleasant company, nothing serious, nothing to leave behind.

Chapter 5

A Government Paid Tour

of the Pacific

Training came to an end, and we began what we joked was our government paid tour of the Pacific: Tarawa, Saipan, Tinian, Eniwetok. We had a base camp at Camp Tarawa in Hawaii, which had been taken in battle in late November, 1943. Capturing Tarawa had been a necessary component of the plan to secure the Marshall Islands. Starting with the battle for Tarawa, the U.S. Amphibious forces faced serious Japanese resistance. Until the attack on Iwo Jima, this pattern of Japanese resistance to U.S. Invading forces in the Pacific islands continued.

General Holland Smith was given the order to take Iwo Jima in October, 1944. We learned of the plan for attack shortly after, as well as the importance of this mission. Seizure of Iwo Jima was to provide a landing base for the long range bombers that would be used to attack the heart of the Japanese empire. We had trained and trained for this operation; its final disclosure was a relief because we could fix a place and mission to what we were doing.

My assignment was Regiment Chemical Warfare Officer functioning as Assistant Regimental Operations Officer for the 28th Regiment. My immediate superiors were Major Oscar Peatross, of Raleigh, NC and Capt. Fred Haynes, a Texan. Over the prolonged training and waiting, we learned little bits about each others' lives, information that worked like a numbered connect-the-dots to provide an overall outline of the person. The interior of that picture, the character of that person, could rarely be known so well as it was in combat when descriptions were provided by the acts each Marine committed. But one of the things I had learned from Peatross was that he was a graduate of North Carolina State University and had played baseball on the 1939 baseball team. I shared with him the highlight of my baseball career, when I played on the junior high baseball team. We arrived for an away game only to find our catcher managed to get lost on the way. When no one else would volunteer to play catcher, I stepped up. The missing catcher had all the gear with him, so I played without a face mask, catcher's mitt, or chest protector. Several times the batter would swing and miss the ball; I would move to catch it and miss. At the end of the three innings, the game was called on account of rain. I never tried to play catcher again. Peatross and I laughed over my having taken one for the team, taken several actually. He was a super guy who turned out to be one of the most decorated men in the Marine Corps, later becoming Major General in charge of Parris Island. The other man in the operations section was Captain Fred Haynes, who later became Commanding General at Camp LeJeune, NC.

The Fifth Division was ordered overseas and based on the big Island of Hawaii. Our camp was named Tarawa, high up the mountains between two inactive volcanoes. When we boarded the ship for Iwo Jima, I was not unusually concerned for my life. The training had been intense and complete but my focus was entirely on killing Japanese instead of being killed, though I think few of us believed we would survive the attack. Nobody talked of such matters though; we were all joking and bravado. We had to be.

In fact, I was mainly concerned about two things: first, letting the Marine Corps down, and second, letting my family down. It was not that I saw myself as any hero; I feared certain things. Fear has to do with circumstances and personality. I had only one regret that I can remember – should I die, I would never have a chance to get married and have a family. That was the thing that concerned me most about getting killed. I knew who I was and what I believed in and where I was going.

I was always more concerned about doing my duty. It was duty, honor, and country that were paramount in my mind. I wanted the enlisted men to respect my example. As officers, we would take exposure to enemy fire as an example for the men. On Iwo Jima the dividing lines between forward and back lines would be so blurred, the officers were shoulder to shoulder with the enlisted men the entire time. There was little question of what a Marine officer would do versus an enlisted Marine, or if orders would be followed. We would advance side by side and take fire across the depth and breadth of every rank alike, though we didn't know that yet. We only knew Iwo Jima was our target, that the island was a key piece of the attack on the Japanese mainland, and that so far the Japanese had put up serious resistance to the previous assaulting forces with the first wave hitting the beach.

We sailed aboard the USS Talladega, a 12,450 ton Haskell class attack transport ship newly commissioned in October 1944. She was 455' from bow to stern and 62' across at her widest point. She was big. It took 56 officers and 480 enlisted men to run her, with troop accommodations for another 86 officers and 1,475 enlisted men. On the day we set out, we had a full complement. From Camp Tarawa, we sailed to Honolulu and then to Saipan and on to Iwo Jima. The trip stretched across days that felt overly long. While I had daily duties and briefings, the main task for myself and the other officers seemed to be keeping the enlisted ranks aboard sane and occupied so that doubts and fear and boredom, the never-ending boredom, didn't eat them alive. We played bridge till the cards were dog-eared and flimsy, sunbathed on deck, and shared stories of what and whom we had left behind. Music played over the loudspeaker: Frank Sinatra, the Andrews Sisters, and Bing Crosby, etc. The music was like a curtain that held behind it all that was familiar, alive, and sure in our lives. Quarters were cramped and tempers flared easily. Even in the officers' quarters, our sleeping bunks were stacked four high. I read when I could, checking books out from the ship's library, such as Dante's *Inferno* and *A Tale of Two Cities* by Charles Dickens. I consumed any real-life adventure stories I could find, and I still had time on my hands.

The waters of the Pacific passed beneath us, beside us, as far one could see. We talked about returning home because the plans made us believe in the possibility of going home, the specter of an appointment would anchor our life to that future point and force us through the coming battle alive. For me, it was the 1945 Rose Bowl. "I'll be there," I told the men, "no matter what." "Lt. Henderson's going to the Rose Bowl," they cheered me on. "Any takers on that bet?" I believed I'd get there; I believed it as much as I could.

Standing on the deck of the Talladega the night before D-Day, I looked into the inky mass that was the sky overhead, dotted with thousands of stars. Looking down from above, we must have appeared much the same, with the running lights of over hundreds of ships floating against the rolling velvet black of the ocean, spread in all directions. I lit up a cigarette and couldn't help thinking of how I had waited for an occasion like this since childhood. My friends and I would wage make believe war with other clubs or groups of boys we had organized in the neighborhood, attacking them in their forts or fearlessly defending our own. Elaborate mazes we had excavated and camouflaged served as headquarters and outlying forts. We used weapons we had fabricated, such as wooden swords and pistols, working hard to stick to the strategy our elected leader had determined. We received a time of attack and individual orders necessary to ensure victory. After the hour-long skirmishes, we would return to our forts to assess the outcome and eat some treats. An open fire pit allowed us to cook indoors with the smoke rising through a make-shift chimney. Smoke still settled in the room, leaving us a little queasy and muddle-headed. But the pork and beans, Vienna sausages, crackers, and Pepsi were eaten with the gusto of men having faced death.

My imagination for such attacks was fed by the stories I read in books and newspapers. I particularly liked stories of the Wild West with its intrepid frontiersmen and resourceful women. The hardships they encountered on the edge of the known world had me imagining some kindred spirit in myself. How I wanted to be a grown man then, worthy of such stories, worthy of my father's expectations and opinions.

Iwo Jima was less than a few hours away. How many others sat smoking cigarettes, thinking back, thinking forward, finding some time in their mind that was a refuge from the here and now? I took a drag off the cigarette that had steadily burned down in the wind. We used to watch our fathers smoke cigars and cigarettes as they talked about whatever grown men talked about – money, crops, sports, politics. They smoked, so we smoked to show we could be men too. What causes the longing to grow up faster than needed? Is it because our world is filled with no, don't, can't, and wait until you're older?

Our smokes were primitive at first, a weed we collected called rabbit tobacco that could be crushed and rolled into a cigarette, using purloined cigarette papers. Those weren't very good, though, so we graduated to cigars in the form of discarded butts that our fathers threw out. Hiding behind one of the outbuildings, we would smoke and grin, laughing at whoever choked the most.

One afternoon, after smoking the remains of one of my father's cigars, our family went into town to shop. With the shopping completed, we headed for a treat – ice cream. For my family, this was a rare treat indeed. I savored each lick of my cone, trying to make it last as long as possible on my tongue. It wasn't long before I started to feel light-headed and my stomach leaden. I could taste the memory of the cigars, and the smoke curled in my stomach, turning the rich ice cream rancid. I doubled over in misery, feeling like I was going to get sick. I must have looked as green on the outside as I felt on the inside because my mother, flushed with concern, insisted we visit the doctor on the way home. After several minutes of questioning by the doctor, I confessed to smoking the cigar. Perhaps if the doctor knew what had caused it, he would know a way to make it better, I reasoned. Instead, I kept the upset stomach and he had a good laugh. The humor escaped my mother and father, at least in front of me, and my father applied the board of adjustment (a belt in this case) to my backside. I gave up cigars in favor of ice cream and my behind.

On board the Talladega, I took one last draw from the cigarette, exhaled deeply and flicked my cigarette butt into the void over the side of the ship. The smoke whirled away. I was tired of thinking. I knew in the end that my life was in God's hands, and no amount of worrying over outcomes could change that. I could only do my best. I left the rail and returned below deck.

Chapter 6

D-Day on Iwo Jima

W E STOLE INTO THE WATERS OFF THE southeast side of Iwo Jima in the early morning hours of February 19, 1945. Aerial assaults on the island began at 0200, not so much to hit targets but to keep the Japs awake and on edge. If some were killed, even better. H-hour was 0900. We rose around 0330 and were treated to a breakfast reminiscent of a gladiator send-off. In the days of the gladiators, their guards would shout before sending them off to battle, "We salute you who are about to die." We were served steak and eggs for breakfast; I imagined it was the crew's way of saying, "We salute you who are about to die." The Talladega was outfitted with landing craft that rolled out from ports on the side of the ship. At 0700, the first of the troop transports were loaded and ready to go. The men sat with their packs at their feet. This was a necessity because if the landing craft went down on the way to the beach, the lifebelt the men wore would inflate. If they wore their packs already, the weight would tip them head-down in the water. Some sat smoking; most were joking. The light mood belied the real fear and tension that could be felt like body heat coming off the men.

Being on the headquarters' staff, I was on the control boat with the commanding officer Colonel Liversedge. Amtracs and other landing craft were circling in the water, performing a bizarre aquatic ballet that would put each assault wave in proper position for attack. I listened to orders from the command staff and relayed them, watching along with the others through field glasses. The hundreds of ships arrayed themselves mostly along the eastern coast. The entire complement of vessels in the attack force would stretch seven miles north to south and 25 miles back from Iwo Jima. Aircraft screamed overhead; bombs let loose from U.S. Planes, like the B-24 Liberator, the P-38 Lightning, and the PBY Catalina, exploded across the island; and smoke obscured a good part of our target. Battleships and smaller warships fired continually on targets on the beach and further inland in preparation for the beach landing. Not one shot was returned by Japanese fire from the island, although a few Japanese planes flew overhead.

The 28th regiment was ordered to land on the south end of Iwo closest to Mt. Suribachi, an area designated Green Beach. These troops would land about 1,200 feet from the base of Mt. Suribachi. Iwo Jima was the most heavily fortified island anywhere in the Pacific and had priority over defense materials for years. There was no mistaking the fact that attacking Iwo Jima was viewed as an incursion into the Japanese homeland. The Emperor himself selected the commander to lead Iwo's defense, General Kuribayashi. He had an illustrious career in the Japanese military and was Head of the Imperial Guards. Kuribayashi had a brilliant defense for the island, though of course we did not know any of this at the time. Fortifications had begun in mid-1944, as the Japanese expected our attack much earlier. Thousands of pillboxes and fortifications had been constructed and covered over so they were indistinguishable from the natural landscape. Miles of tunnels were dug and connected, and the entire system was wired for communication between the fortifications. Mt. Suribachi, rising 560 feet above the beach at the south end of the island, had been heavily armed with troops and weapons, having the best vantage point for troops to saturate the beaches with gun and mortar fire. None of this could be seen, and, for the most part, the Japanese held to a strict order not to retaliate against any incursions, so relying on gunfire to locate possible targets was ineffective.

Investigations at the end of the war would reveal the driving force behind Kuribayashi's plan for fortification. Japan had few resources with which to defend Iwo Jima and never expected any outcome other than U.S. Success. As a result, the only option was to prolong the battle, when it finally occurred, as long as possible with as high a casualty rate for the U.S. Troops as possible in order to provide time for Japan to prepare the mainland for invasion. Up until this point, most attacks on Pacific Islands were characterized by the first and second waves receiving the brunt of the attack. The Japanese lost a lot of troops that way, which we liked. While it was tough for the first few waves, we would kill a lot of Japs. They would come in waves yelling and screaming like a bunch of wild men; it was easy to kill them. Kuribiyashi's plan was to wait, to hold off firing until several waves had hit the beach.

We didn't know this until after, so we ordered in wave after wave of amtracs and LCDs full of troops, with the first landing on the beach at 0859, a minute before H-hour. Nothing happened, that is to say we didn't see the expected retaliatory gunfire. All eyes were trained on the beach, waiting. We decided the aerial attacks leading up to the invasion had been more successful than anticipated. Aircraft were still circling overhead, dropping bombs, and the battleships firing on Iwo aimed further inland. Soon after the first battalion hit the beach, Captain Gilland, the 1st Battalion operations officer, was killed when a kamikaze pilot hit the amtrac he was on. A call came in from Colonel Butterfield, who was the commanding officer of the first battalion, requesting Colonel Liversedge, our regimental commander, to send me down as his operations officer. I must admit I felt safer in the control boat. Nevertheless, I transferred from the control boat to a landing craft and hit Green Beach with the fourth wave to join the 1st Battalion.

Kuribiyashi held off on the first, second, and third waves because he wanted as many troops on the beach as possible before he ordered the firing to commence. As I watched from the landing craft, our men were hitting the beaches and nothing was happening.

We landed, followed by the fifth and sixth waves, which took about 30-45 minutes from when I had boarded the landing craft. That was when all hell broke loose. The noise was indescribable except to say that it was all around and overwhelming. I heard it and felt it. Thousands of guns were zeroed in on the beach, blasting away at the same time. We had six to eight thousand men on the beach at that point, most of them struggling to take just a few steps forward. The beach was very difficult to navigate because it was volcanic sand or ash, which was like trying to run through shelled corn. As soon as I landed and started to move, my reaction was the same as every other Marine's – what the hell am I running on? It was like running in place. There was no traction and any hole we dug filled right back up as fast as we scooped it out. Directly in front of us, the beach rose for 12 to 15 feet with this volcanic ash before the first terrace could be reached. Behind us, the troops continued landing and unloading; bombed and disabled vehicles and landing craft began to pile up along the beach. All around us was gunfire.

In one moment, the action moved from hectic but controlled to chaotic and instinctual. The beach erupted with gunfire, mortars, and artillery. Kuribayashi had given the order to fire. I heard all the noise at once but in distinct pieces. The gunfire sounded in a continuous rat-a-tat-tat; the bullets pinged against the metal amtracs, tanks, and jeeps. I could hear the tank treads spinning, moving the tanks not forward but down into the sand. Soft thuds of bullets tearing flesh sounded all around us, and the voices of men calling out orders were stopped short so the sentences were completed only by my mind. Mortars approached with a whine that descended in pitch the closer they came. When they exploded, they sent men or parts of them flying by. The volcanic ash, thrown into the air by the explosions, rained down over us with a bite. Bodies and parts of them landed with dull thuds against the beach. Men dropped to the ground for cover or dropped to the ground for good.

We were subject to enfilade fire, which sent the number of casualties skyrocketing. Direct fire is firing straight ahead; enfilade fire is firing down a line, so there is a much greater chance of hitting a target. Fire came in from both flanks, making it difficult to move off the beach. After my initial landing and the onslaught of gunfire, I scrambled as best I could up the rise. I turned to return to the beach for something, I can't remember what, when I saw Buttermilk standing in the sand. "Buttermilk," I shouted, "get up and go. Don't just stand there. Move it!" Buttermilk was a young Marine who had earned his nickname because he was too young to order drinks in a bar. He ordered buttermilk instead. I didn't know him personally since I had just joined the battalion, but I recognized he was with our outfit. I knew we had to move men off the beach as quickly as possible, so I shouted for him to move. I thought, *that's weird, he's dug himself waist deep into the sand. Why did he do that?* It took a moment, me yelling at Buttermilk to move and Buttermilk staring at me, before I realized that the lower part of his body had been blown off. He very slowly toppled over. At moments like that, there was little choice but to move on or die, paralyzed with fear, confusion, and anger.

There were many Buttermilks, dead before you had a chance to know them or even be properly introduced. Then there were the men like Corporal Stein, who were so gung-ho about killing it didn't seem right. He couldn't wait to see combat. He had appropriated a machine gun from an airplane, an air-cooled machine gun that was lighter than the water-cooled guns we carried. He had modified it so he could hold it in his hand. Where our automatic rifles could shoot 20 rounds and our M1s could shoot 8 rounds, that machine gun could shoot several hundred rounds in one clip. It was very effective. The Corporal was having a ball with it. As we moved inland, he approached one pillbox and the Japanese came out in an attempt to escape, which in itself was unusual. After the attack was over, we counted 16 Japanese that he had killed at that one spot. He finally ran out of ammunition and went back to the beach for more. There were pillboxes everywhere, mounds of concrete five feet thick and covered with dirt so they couldn't be detected. He went back to the beach several times, and several times he would assist a corpsman with carrying a wounded marine back to the beach for medical aid. I helped him carry one Marine to an aid station. At one point when the Corporal was charging across the island, his weapon was shot out of his hand and he was killed. I must admit to being divided when it came to his actions. The situation at Iwo Jima called for heroics, for uncommon valor among men who had trained hard and long and rose to the occasion. But there was a fine line between heroism and recklessness that was more readily felt than known intellectually. Recklessness could kill a lot of Japanese, but it could kill the Marine too.

Our battalion's mission was to move across the island, bisecting it so Mt. Suribachi would be cut off from the rest of the island. General Kuribiyashi had designed an ingenious system of caves, with 16 or so miles of underground tunnels spread across three different levels connecting the mountain with the rest of the island. Soldiers would pop up in one cave, then go down and pop up again in another. Kuribiyashi's command post was situated 75 feet underground and therefore went untouched by the bombardment. Frankly, most of the caves were not touched by the bombing.

We bisected that bloody island by 10:30 a.m. On D-day. We staggered in increasingly reduced numbers, grouping together, checking over the map, and sending men out, "Go, go, go!" a few at a time. We fought every step of the way. Platoon leader, Lt. Frank Waight, was the first to lead his platoon across to the west beach. He bypassed a lot of fortifications and ran through a Jap Command Post. The casualties were terrible as we were at a distinct disadvantage. Guns were firing and artillery rained down from Mt. Suribachi, while at the same time guns and artillery streamed across the terrain from pillboxes all around us. No terrain seemed available that was not in the sights of some Japanese gunner or reachable by some mortar fire. Our own big guns, wedged into quickly constructed holes dug out and reinforced with sandbags, fired on Suribachi's emplacements as best they could be pinpointed. Tanks not mired down on the beach or already selected as a viable target for mortar fire attempted to take out whatever targets they could sight or that we called in. The gunboats and battleships off the beach maintained a steady barrage covering the mountain and hitting targets inland. Still, our troops dropped in record numbers. If the gunfire seemed constant, the call "Corpsmen!" was ever-present also.

We reported 80% casualties while making our way across the island. Fortunately, that percentage was lowered when men who had been separated from their unit later returned. With the uneven terrain, the constant gunfire, the loss of men, the smoke from ammunitions, and the noise, it wasn't hard to be separated from your unit. After completing our cut across the base of the island, we regrouped for the attack on Mt. Suribachi.

Chapter 7

Mt. Suribachi

REGROUPING TO ATTACK MT. SURIBACHI meant finding reinforcements. The 1st Battalion was so shot up that they sent the 2nd and 3rd Battalion in to take Suribachi. We struggled there for three days – three days to cover the 1,200 feet from where we had landed on Green Beach to the base of Mt. Suribachi. Every foot we had to fight for by hand — this was D day +3, which was February 23. Tanks and heavy guns gradually crept closer as targets on the mountain were discovered and heavily bombarded with gunfire and mortars.

Colonel Johnson commanded the 2nd Battalion. The old man, Colonel Liversedge, sent a message to Johnson, "Take that mountain." Johnson replied, "Colonel, I can't find my men." Liversedge said to him, "You take that mountain and if you are not off in five minutes, you are up for a general court marshal." Colonel Liversedge was a no-nonsense leader – fair but tough.

We set up a command post at the base and sent two initial groups of men to ferret out and destroy any resistance. The Japanese had roughly 1,600 men defending Mt. Suribachi, but few were encountered as the two units made their way to the top. Johnson then selected Lt. George Schrier, a decorated Marine who had served on Bougainville and Guadalcanal, to lead the assault. Johnson told Schrier to take a detail, but since his platoon was all shot up, he had to take some men from the machine gun and mortar sections. About 35-40 men started up Suribachi. The progress was slow and arduous over the volcanic rock. Just before he left, Colonel Johnson said, "Here, take this and put it up when you get there." It was the flag in his knapsack, which he took out and handed to Schrier. At 1020 on February 23, Schrier and his men raised the flag over Iwo Jima. I know this because I sent the message back to HQ from the command post at the base of Suribachi.

That was the first flag, though. The Secretary of the Navy, Admiral James Forrestal, who came out from Washington to observe, landed at the beach near the base of Mt. Suribachi. He sent a message to Colonel Johnson, "Sir, I want that flag."
Colonel Johnson said, "To hell with him. This flag belongs to the 2nd Battalion, and he won't get this

flag." I stood by, watching, wondering what the outcome of this struggle would be. Someone said, "Colonel, why don't we get another flag and send it up there and give him that one. We'll keep the real one." With a big grin on his face, Johnson sent a runner back down to the beach to find a bigger flag, which was sent to the top of Mt. Suribachi for the second flag raising. The famous picture that Joe Rosenthal took was of the second flag. When that flag went up, the Marines on the whole island could see it. There was a cheer that included the ships off shore and sounded like an exuberant crowd of football fans. The convoy was over 800 ships, seven miles long and twenty-six miles wide. Colonel Johnson sent Admiral Forrestal the second flag, and he kept the first. We had been assigned to take the southern end of the island, and that job was completed. However, we were still a long way from finishing the job.

It's like this: *When I was a child, I spoke and thought and reasoned as a child does. But when I grew up, I put away childish things. Now we see things imperfectly as in a poor mirror, but then we will see everything with perfect clarity. All that I know now is partial and incomplete, but then I will know everything completely, just as God knows me now. 1 Cor 13:11-12*

Chapter 8

Securing Iwo Jima

O VER 22,000 JAPANESE PROTECTED the island when we landed. After 10 days of fighting, there were still 16,000 alive. We could not see them or get to them, and we lost a lot of men trying. While the beach had been difficult to navigate, at least it had been fairly even. Proceeding inward and northward over the island, we encountered broken terrain with deep trenches and ravines. The smell of sulfur was everywhere. Iwo Jima translated was literally Sulfur Island. The volcano, long dormant, still kept the island bed warm. In our foxholes we sat with our bottoms warmed and our tops wet and cold.

Our troops had run into heavy opposition in the north because we had run the Japs on Mt. Suribachi back into their tunnels. Some of the men had found the communications line that linked Mt. Suribachi to Kuribayashi's command post and severed it during our attack. With no way to communicate, the Japs panicked and fled through the tunnels north. The terrain made attacking very difficult. The 28th Regiment was ordered to attack the north side of the island. We took the left sector of the north end, where we encountered our most fierce fighting and the greatest number of casualties.

Every inch of ground covered and captured was fought and paid for in such staggering numbers it was hard to find the men to replace those who had died. We would attack and capture a ridge and move down the reverse slope, exposed. When we made it to the bottom of the ravine, the Japs would fire at us from up above. The loss of life continued at a furious pace. As operations officers, I remember at one point we were sent five replacement officers. They were assigned to front line outfits; one hour later, three were casualties. Sometimes replacements were not sent to the front lines until they were on the island for a day or two. Their esprit de corps was so high; they often took risks they shouldn't. They were not combat experienced and didn't know how much of a risk to take.

We continued ten or twelve days of tough fighting before I finally lost someone I had known like a brother. Walking away was not so easy. On March 17, we were two-thirds of the way up the island, attacking hill 362, which was a Jap stronghold and strategically located. The 26th Marines were on our right. Somehow we moved ahead of them or they fell behind; either way it ended up we had a gap in the line. One of our company leaders, Capt. Wilkins, was leading the attack. He was one of my closest friends. He was a physical giant, but sort of a puppy dog of an individual. I could say he was a great guy with all that implies, but it says everything and nothing at the same time. He was the kind of guy I would want to fight beside. When Captain Wilkins' radio man was wounded, we were left with no contact. I made my way to his CP to see where they were and what was going on. A gap in the line could be disastrous as the enemy could pass through and elude us or divide and attack us. We had to determine if there was a gap and figure out how to fix it.

I crawled into the hole close to Wilkins, but I didn't realize he was at the front of his line leading his men. We were attempting to talk when small arms fire became intense along with mortar and artillery shells. They had that high-pitched whine that descended the closer they fell to earth. When I looked around to see what happened to Captain Wilkins, I could tell by the look of him that he had taken several mortal wounds. I called for a Corpsman. I couldn't do anything but watch him die. He could not speak, but his eyes expressed his thanks.

He took a couple of gurgling breaths, and then he was gone.

The anger that sprang up in me was sudden and all-consuming, like nothing I had ever felt. It was a rage that left me shaking. This pagan nation, in order to satisfy their ego and gratify their ungodly Emperor, had caused thousands of men to lose their lives, Americans as well as Japanese. My anger had me nearly leaping from the foxhole to kill anyone I could see. But thank God, I restrained myself. I had brought my emotions under enough control to remember what I was about – finding a way to close the gap between our two units. I crawled from the foxhole and escaped to the battalion command post about 300 feet behind us.

This type of activity continued for several days. The routine of every day kept at bay my feelings over Wilkins' death. There would be an artillery barrage. We would advance inch by inch, foot by foot, with vicious hand to hand combat. The nights were the worst; it was wet, cold, and miserable. Iwo Jima was a Pacific island, but in February it was no Palm Beach. Every night the Japanese would infiltrate our ranks. They would sneak in with knives and bayonets to slit throats or mortally wound a Marine; they'd disappear before the wounded and dead were discovered. We fired star shells to illuminate the terrain and Japanese soldiers on the move, but we couldn't see them all.

One night, in the half-sleep we all shared, something woke me - a noise, a sensation. We were hyper alert, even as we sat curled up in the hole, trying to keep exhaustion at bay. All my senses were focused outward, like antennae. Something made me open my eyes and look up. Standing above the foxhole next to me I saw a ghostly figure. The Jap soldier had his sword raised to decapitate the Marine in the next foxhole. In one step I was on him. I jammed my bayonet in and twisted it, then I pulled it out and jammed it in again. When he fell on his back, I jammed my bayonet in again for good measure. He never cried out, and I don't remember if I did when I attacked. I went back to my hole and spent the night in the deceptive silence. That nightmare played out every night in and around one foxhole or another. We didn't talk much about them and thanks went without saying. Sleep was elusive, but the vigilance required to stay alive was what really drained us. In the morning, I woke up and searched the dead soldier's body. I found a letter, which our interpreter read for us. The Japanese soldier had been writing to his wife back home. Their son had been born in his absence; a photo was in his pocket. He was writing to express how proud he was. I confess it did not move my heart. It should have, but it did not. I only wished I had killed him sooner because I may have saved some of my buddies' lives.

During the days we moved northward, heroism was everywhere. On one occasion, while negotiating a trench, five or six of us ducked and crawled our way ahead, a corporal up in front of us. The trench zigzagged. A group of Japs appeared ahead, and from around the curve, they threw a grenade at us. The corporal pushed it into the volcanic ash with his foot. When they threw another one, the corporal realized he didn't have the time to pick it up and throw it back at them or push it into the ground. So he fell on it. The rest of us dove for cover. We heard a muffled explosion. We hurried to his side, and bless my soul, by some miracle he was not dead. He was conscious and talking. Doc Bradley, a Navy corpsman asked, "Why in the hell did you do that?" He said simply, "I did it to protect you guys." That was the kind of commitment we had for each other - the kind of commitment that accounted for the fact that many of us did survive.

Combat had terrible moments, but it had high moments as well. I experienced a spiritual emotion while fighting on that island that was subordinate only to my experience with God and my family. Although there were many dark moments, there were encouraging times when we saw self-sacrifice, duty, and honor demonstrated in ways that my youth could not have imagined. I thought of David, fleeing from Saul and hiding in caves. I thought of Psalm 23, for surely I could be no closer to the valley of the shadow of death than right here on Iwo Jima.

I reminded myself that the Lord was my shepherd and He would provide me with the still waters and green pastures, moments of rest and restoration in even the most tragic of circumstances. I also knew that God's love did not mean I would not suffer. I might even die, but He would be with me. Knowing that gave me comfort to face my fears: fear of the unknown, fear of what lay over the next rise, fear for the men serving beside me.

Like David, I found that my cup overflowed with blessings as I watched men sacrifice their lives for fellow Marines, for Americans thousands of miles away, and for shared beliefs. It was a grace from God to have the living Word of the Bible remind me of what I was fighting for – not to save my life, because my life had already been ransomed and paid for, but to stand as a witness to God no matter what circumstances I found myself in.

Rare moments of quiet afforded us the opportunity for some semblance of normal to invade the waking nightmare we found ourselves inhabiting. We sat snug against a sandbagged wall, fresh from securing a tiny patch of the island and a minute or two from moving forward. The sound of a match being lit rasped against the singular moment of silence: the match lighting, the sucking on the cigarette butt to draw the flame in, and the sound of the tobacco crackling to life. That cigarette was like a small wrapped morsel of relaxation, and we drew it in as deep as the warmth of summer breezes back home.

"The 27th got three Jap flags. Can you believe that? We ain't got one yet today," complained one of the privates. I always had some bet going, some competition to keep the men's attention focused on something else besides the death around us, and their fear, fatigue, and hunger. We'd bet in training on when my boots would wear out (I wore those boots until the soles were flapping so much they had a language of their own); we competed for who would capture the most Jap flags; and we judged whose plans for home were the best worth making it home for.

"Lt. Henderson, was that your stomach, Sir?"

I laughed because we should've had a competition over whose stomach could growl the loudest. It had been a day or two since we had had any C-rations. C-rations were a far cry from a tasty meal, but they we preferred to less tasteful K-rations.

"It was either my stomach or the dirt on my body has come to life," I said. The comment was a joke, but the dirt wasn't. We were crawling through the ash, sleeping in the ash, and showering in the ash every time a mortar exploded nearby. I itched and smelled, the only consolation being I wasn't the only one. The last bath I'd had was a week ago, and "bath" was a bit of misnomer. The bath consisted of heating water in our helmets. We would wash with a cloth, being careful to not waste a drop. Water was a precious commodity on the island. Huge lister bags holding 60 gallons or so were transported to the rear of each unit where a designated Marine would fill canteens. We could survive for a time without the food, but the water was as necessary as the cigaretts.

Finally, on March 26 we secured the island. "Secure" was a relative term because many of the Japanese were still hidden underground. Clean-up involved finding and taking, if possible alive, all of them. Even after we secured the island, those remaining Japanese popped up from holes and continued to kill Marines as we passed. They knew they would never survive and that we would take the island. Aside from delaying the invasion against the Japanese mainland as long as possible, they hoped to make us pay such a heavy price in casualties that the people back home would be upset and demand their boys be brought home. It almost worked. Our casualties were high enough to cause us to reconsider whether to invade the mainland or sue for peace.

We policed our area and picked up our gear. We salvaged a lot of equipment and material and prepared to be evacuated and sail back to our base camp. We left behind our dead, a lot of blood, and our youthfulness. As we struggled down the road to the beaches, we looked like a rag tag bunch. We were a miserable looking outfit that was a mere shadow of the force that had landed a little over a month earlier. These men had endured 36 days of intense direct conflict. No, not conflict. That's too white-washed a word. Intense direct, deadly combat. In other long battles, the skirmish would go on for a few days and then back off, but not on Iwo. I had not shaved for six weeks. We were crusted with sweat, rain, and dried volcanic ash. Only our mothers could have loved us at this point. Our eyes were sunken from lack of sleep and blurred from the horrors we had seen.

As we moved down the beach, we walked by the 5th Marine division cemetery. I noted a change in the men. They started to march, straight-backed with heads held high. They formed up themselves without an order, and instead of stumbling, they were marching. Those who were limping also began to march as best they could. When we arrived at the cemetery, everyone was standing ramrod straight. There was not one Marine limping. A sense of awe and reverence covered us. As I left, I saw an epitaph written on an ammunitions box. As best as I can remember, it read: "When you go home, tell them for us and say, for your tomorrows, we gave our todays." We stumbled off the beach and into the landing craft.

We had no docks, so we were transported to the ships by small boats. When we arrived alongside the ships, some were too weak to climb aboard. Big husky sailors held the weak and wounded in their arms like children and carried them aboard. When my battalion landed on February 19, we had 895 enlisted men and officers. A total of 304 replacements were added to our ranks for a total of 1,195 men. When we came off the island, we had suffered 784 casualties. It took 22 ships to bring the 5th Division to Iwo Jima; it only took eight ships to take us home.

The invading Marines were awarded 27 Medals of Honor. There never was an outfit in military history awarded that many Medals of Honor for a single engagement. Many of them were awarded posthumously. We boarded ship and most of the men slept for three days. I did not have that opportunity. The old man, Colonel Liversedge, said, "Henderson, you need this experience." I was assigned the duty of writing the operations report for the 1st battalion, 28th Marines. I spent over half the trip recording those events by hand, and a clerk would type them up for the Colonel to read. The increasing distance between our ship and Iwo Jima failed to lessen the horror of those 36 days. For some reason, I kept the story of Colonel Johnson's flag to myself. Three days after the flag raising, Colonel Johnson was blown up on Iwo Jima. I've heard the flag is in a Marine Corp museum in Washington, DC.

We went back to our base camp at Camp Tarawa in Hawaii. After settling back in, we were given the opportunity for some R&R. There was an air base, and several times during the day planes would fly from the big island of Hawaii to Honolulu on Oahu. When I was returning by plane from a week in Honolulu, another plane had been cleared for take off just as we were landing. Our planes collided, but both pilots were able to land the damaged planes. I thought how ironic and sad it would be to have survived combat only to be killed in a plane crash in a peaceful environment on the way back from a brief vacation.

Replacement troops arrived, and we began the training cycle all over again. This time we trained to attack the mainland of Japan. The losses at Iwo spurred us on in the same way that Pearl Harbor prompted us to enlist in the first place. We planned for months, and in the final hours, as we were loading our ships, we received news on August 12th that the Japanese would surrender. General Rocky, the 5th Division Commander, immediately stopped all training exercises. We always lost men in the training exercises, and frankly, we had already lost enough.

War is an ugly thing, but not the ugliest of things. The decayed and degraded state of moral and patriotic feeling, which thinks that nothing is worth war, is much worse. The person who has nothing for which he is willing to fight, nothing which is more important than his own personal safety, is a miserable creature and has no chance of being free unless made and kept so by the exertions of better men than himself.
- *John Stuart Mills*

Chapter 9

Occupied Japan

T HE 5TH DIVISION WASN'T HEADED home yet. The commanders of the war in the Pacific said we had studied the terrain and knew the Japanese so well that we were being sent in as the occupation force. We considered it a privilege to be the first troops to set foot on occupied Japan, a conquered land.

I wouldn't have thought it possible to have stepped out of the frying pan and into the fire after my experiences on Iwo, but there we were. As we traveled to Sasebo, a storm kicked up like nothing I had experienced before even though we were on the outer edge. If I had not known excitement before, I really knew it then. The storm subsided and we were intact, but it would take a spell to shake off the experience.

The war had been over only a short time. We had experienced the fanaticism of the Japanese fighting firsthand. Samurai had sworn to defend their country to the death. I was worried, and with good reason I thought, whether they had all received word of their surrender. With my concerns nagging at me, we exchanged the rolling pitch of the ship for a long march to our landside destination. When we marched down the streets of Sasebo, which had 400,000 people, my concerns resurfaced. I searched the montage of faces that blurred by, their foreignness making their expressions even more inscrutable. *Which one,* I wondered, *had not heard yet that the war was over, or had heard but chosen to ignore the order of surrender?* I could not have made a more obvious target.

We arrived at Aniouri Naval Barracks, a major naval base. I believed my capacity to be surprised by the Japanese fighting spirit was all but gone. Iwo had shown me the depth of their commitment, but the condition of Aniouri surprised me nonetheless. The devastation was total; there was nothing left. Buildings, vehicles, ships were bombed out and burned up. I was amazed to see what they had fought with in the war. They had nothing that was not broken or in need of repair. The tenacity of the Japanese people, the dedication, struck me anew.

On our initial visit to Sasebo, Lt. John McLean, an interpreter, and I were tasked with taking an inventory of any weapons that could be used in combat.

The first location I visited with Lt. McLean was a large abandoned and foreboding warehouse. John was my interpreter, a smart guy from the Mclean family, both a wealthy and distinguished lineage when family names still counted for a good deal. We were in a little room with no ceiling, just rafters. Though we had not encountered any hostile citizens, the looks on the faces of the Japanese were less than inviting. They had surrendered, but the shame and anger - mostly shame – that they carried because of it was as evident as if they had carried it in a bag on their backs. I did not trust what might happen.

When we were ready to leave, the doors were locked. I strongly objected. The Japanese guard said he had to secure permission from his commander in order to let us leave, and his commander would not be available until the next day. So we settled in for the night. I told John, "You take the first watch."

Later in the night, sometime between an uneasy sleep and skimming the surface of wakefulness, I heard this "bum, bum, bum." John whispered, "I think they are coming at us. I hear them overhead." We focused our flashlight into the rafters where we heard the noise. Wharf rats at least 24 inches long had stormed our warehouse. They looked hungry and big. Their eyes shone down on us.

When the Japanese had abandoned security, the rats had infiltrated the rice stores, but there was nothing left. I looked at the lead rat. He was blinking at me as if he was one leap from dinner. I pulled out my 45 and shot him. With that shot, it seemed WWIII had broken out. The Japanese came out "Yap, Yap, Yap!" The rats bolted, but it took at least an hour to calm the Japanese down. By then, the chances of sleep were like the vague wisps of a good dream.

Overall, our visit did not go well. John came to me after overhearing the Japanese talking.

"Lieutenant, I'm not sure what's going on, but I heard them discussing what they're going to do with us. I don't think they intend to let us go."

The two of us huddled together, trying to figure out options as a great chasm opened between where we were now and our safe return to our barracks. The Japanese guard had been stalling on letting us go, but finally, in the early morning hours, he apologized and released us. Until that moment, we hadn't felt a sense of concern. The Japanese had been very polite and cooperative.

We left Sasebo and moved to the northern sector. We moved among the masses of Japanese, ensuring complete surrender. This involved verifying that any military forces had been disbanded and disarmed. The people accepted their position, and I wondered if they weren't glad that the war was over. Sasebo had been bombed, not as badly as Hiroshima and Nagasaki, but the city had suffered. The nation of Japan had been suffering defeats for some time, which must have signaled some inevitability to the people of Sasebo, like a storm cloud low on the horizon moving in slow and steady. The people were the nation, but they were also individuals, families, shop owners, butchers, fishermen, geisha. I imagined they were eager to return to the business of a daily life not shrouded by the specter of aerial bombings, daily sacrifice, and personal death.

Living in this foreign city was like mixing oil and water. We mingled during the days, smaller groups of soldiers amongst the Japanese, only to settle in the nights completely separate from each other. They were so different—looks, language, demeanor. *Could we be so hospitable if our country were to surrender?*

During the days, I supervised the collection of any type of weapon that could be used to attack the occupation forces. The Japanese had been collecting weapons from their soldiers for surrender to our forces. On one of my inspection tours, we discovered a warehouse that was filled with sabers, every kind from military issue to family heirlooms several hundred years old. We collected a large number to be sent to Marine Corps Headquarters, war booty I suppose. I selected 25 or 30 that I brought back to the States and sent to members of our regiment who had been wounded and relieved of duty. Inscriptions graced many of these sabers, detailing its history, family of origin, or maker. Like all blades, these were two-edged with the history of the Japanese soldier who wielded it written on one side.

I visited Hiroshima too, though I can't say for sure what drew me there – a macabre curiosity, a sense of sadness, a sense of responsibility. Hiroshima was a city surrounded by a circle of hills, similar to ancient Rome. The main road into the city traveled over the crest of one of these hills. As my jeep came over the hilltop, I gazed at a scene of total devastation. Hundreds and hundreds of buildings were destroyed. I saw a few freak phenomena, like one building still standing with everything around it demolished, a lone obscene gesture in the face of the bombings. The streets were crowded with people fleeing the city. Others were coming back to view their homes and collect anything of value.

I thought of the long ago tragedies I had witnessed in my youth - a burned mill village and a small town struck by a tornado. On those occasions, my brother and I had picked through the disaster area looking for treasures, which for us meant coins or unique stamps with interesting postmarks. Propriety and sadness over the tragedy kept us at bay for only so long, as is the case with most children. We ministered to the unfortunate with our mother and father, helping those who had lost everything, until we could stand it no longer and started to look. The tragedy of Hiroshima was so much more incomprehensible because of its magnitude and the fact that I was no longer a child with a child's understanding. It would have taken a hard heart indeed to be unmoved by the desperation, death, and sadness evident in the people and echoed in the land-scape.

The residents of Hiroshima were restricted to what they could take since no one knew the effects of radiation at that point. Although the Japanese people did not express their emotions, their faces all took on a similar look of emptiness around the eyes, a look I had seen before among the residents of towns broken by natural disasters and among my fellow Marines on Iwo Jima. Many of them wandered aim-lessly, their vacuous faces mirroring the ruined land-scape around them. I imagined we had looked the same on Iwo the moment the guns began firing and during the confusion that ensued. We had been trained, though, how to react, how to regroup; and Iwo was not our home. Barely a month had passed since the bomb had been dropped. Most of these people seemed to have suffered injuries, external burns, and then internal injuries from radiation poi-soning. These internal injuries would eat away at them from the inside, the symptoms of which they may only have been beginning to feel. But I knew, from the trauma I had seen on Iwo, the emotional injuries could be far worse. Physical injuries could at least be identified, classified, cared for or cut off. Emotional injuries rattled around like a madman in the attic of one's mind or like a boa wrapped around the heart.

The hospitals were crowded inside, overflowing onto the streets with the sick and dying. I visited one hospital where the sight of the burned and hopeless caused me to turn away. My mind could scarcely comprehend how one bomb could be so devastating over such a large area. Members of my party had reflected on how this capability could change the strategy of war, the realization that relatively few of these bombs could render a nation totally defenseless. It was an awesome and sobering thought.

How far we had come from God's original plan! How can we love an enemy who's killing millions of innocent people? How do we love an enemy we have to kill? I could well understand a person's inability to see God in such a landscape. I had felt it on Iwo Jima, the desire to call out to God as I watched Marines fall in record numbers. I was thankful on Iwo Jima and thankful now as I looked over this city laid low at the hands of my country. What was I thankful for? I was thankful that my father had instilled in me the knowledge of God's goodness and faithfulness in all things. This devastation was not God's plan but a result of sin. I kept repeating that to myself so that knowing it and feeling it were one in the same. As my heart broke over what I saw, I knew that God's heart was breaking as well.

Chapter 10

Heading Home

I N NOVEMBER 1945, OUR TIME WAS finally up. The Marine Corps had developed a policy that a Marine serving earned so many points for specified terms of service. Once the requisite number of points was accrued, the Marine was eligible to go home; I more than qualified. Scuttlebutt had it there was a plane heading stateside. I asked Col. Liversedge about it and he confirmed the rumor.

"Henderson," the old man said, "If you tried, you may be able to secure a seat and get yourself home."

I have to admit to a certain amount of excitement when I heard this. I could be back in the States in a few days instead of the 25-30 days it would take by ship. I thought about it for a while, but in the end I said, "I think I'll pass trying to get on the flight. I've been with these men through a lot, and I just don't feel right about taking the plane back even if I could."

By this time, my unit was like family. The plane bound for the States took off without me. Several days later I was informed that that flight took off but never landed. In fact, that flight was never heard from again. Talk about God's mercy and grace. I gave a prayer of thanks to God for prompting me to stick with my unit.

We boarded ship, and 26 days later we were back in San Diego, California. The day was December 27, 1945. After calling my family to let them know I had made it safely to port, we immediately cleaned up and headed for Los Angeles, heady with relief and a sense of freedom. I was wandering around the Biltmore Hotel lobby with two of my friends who were slightly inebriated when a man addressed us, "Anyone want some tickets to the Rose Bowl?"

I remembered my promise that I'd be at the Rose Bowl this year. I looked at my buddies and said to the man, "We sure would. How much are they?"

He said, "Son, they're yours."

He handed me six tickets to the Rose Bowl. We invited some female friends to go along with us. As I sat in the stands watching USC beat Tennessee 25 to 0, I said another quick prayer for God's providence in seeing me through the last three and a half years. Not only had I returned safe and whole, but I was sitting with friends enjoying a free football game

– an event I could only have dared dream about from Iwo Jima. Now I was actually here.

My last set of orders was to report to Camp LeJeune in North Carolina. With several days travel time allotted to me, I made my first stop in Atlantic City, New Jersey, to resolve some unfinished business of a romantic nature. While I was in college, I had met a young lady who had become an officer in the Women's Army Corps. We'd dated and become engaged before I left for overseas. They say absence makes the heart grow fonder, but in my case, the fondness grew dim despite our correspondence while I was away. I'm not sure what prompted the engagement to begin with, perhaps simply the desire to believe that someone was waiting back home, someone other than family. We got along all right, but there was little real affection to keep the effects of distance at bay. So, when I visited her in Atlantic City, we mutually agreed to go our separate ways.

As I made my way to my parents' home, now in Burlington, NC, where my father had been assigned to a church, I wondered if they would find me different. Physically I was sure I was different since they had not seen me for several years. The flashbacks I had suffered after leaving Iwo Jima had stopped, and my heightened sense of my surroundings, a constant wariness, had gradually diminished. Yet I still wondered what changes they would see between the young college graduate who had left and the battle-hardened Marine who'd returned.

It may have been a different house – a different location - but the warmth of my parents' embrace felt the same. For a moment, I could have been any young man home on holiday. The social rules that governed talking about unpleasantries, even with family, allowed me to leave my combat experiences untouched. They did not ask for details; I didn't offer any. It was enough for them to say, "Welcome home, son. You're doing well?" To which I replied, "I sure am."

My father's prayers at the table were enough to let me know the depth of his gratefulness to God that I was home safe, and my mother's cooking expressed the rest. We filled the remaining time with talk of the family and the community, my father's new post, and my future prospects.

After a few days of visiting with them, I reported to Camp Lejeune. My orders called for me to report to the commanding General of Camp Lejeune and prepare to be mustered out of active duty. I was housed at the Bachelors' Officers Club, where I received a message to report immediately to the General. This was unusual and concerned me. Had something awry been discovered in my records that would jeopardize my being released from active duty? I quickly short-listed the events I thought could be questioned, chief among them a mishap during the transport of the 28th Marines from Japan to California.

I had been standing on the dock overseeing the loading of the Regiment's equipment aboard the ships that would transport us home. One of our tanks was suspended by cables, moving slowly towards the ship. A dock operator had done something that caused the line to jerk violently. I can remember that metal warbling sound of the cables after they gave way and the interval of silence that signaled trouble. Time had frozen for just that moment, all eyes glued to the tank. Down it went with a great splash into the harbor and collective gasps came from anyone who witnessed the spectacle.

I could just imagine the Marine Corps holding me responsible for that tank. Equipment was taken very seriously in the Marines, and tanks weren't cheap. I worried that I might be looking at the Navy brig for the next twenty years, a thought that made the walk to the Commanding General's office a long and un- happy one.

I was ushered into the General's office, where I snapped to attention before his desk, saluted, and said, "Captain Henderson reporting as ordered, sir."

"At ease, Captain."

"Sir, if I might ask, is there something wrong with my papers? I. . ." I cast about for some way to ask about the problem without volunteering any infor- mation.

"Oh, no. No problems, Captain. Quite the con- trary. I received a call from Colonel Liversedge.

Had nothing but good things to say about you. He told me you were considering the Marines as a career, and he thought I should offer you the opportunity to apply for regular duty."

I hoped my relief didn't show too much. "Oh, well, thank you, sir. I sure appreciate Col. Liversedge's willingness to back me for regular duty. I've spent a good deal of time thinking about this though. I've never really been an adult citizen, sir. I'd like to give civilian life a try. I'd still like to serve in the Marine Reserves, if there's a spot."

"That'll have to do then," he replied. We talked a bit more about Iwo and Sasebo before I was free to go. I left his office and active duty, though I stayed with a reserve regiment for another 12 years.

When the Korean conflict began a few years later, I applied to be reactivated. I was the commander of a reserve company in Greensboro, NC. I wrote Marine Corps Headquarters a letter and did not get an answer. I sent them a wire and did not get an answer. Finally, I went to Washington, and Congressman Chatham agreed to go to bat for me. Finally, I was told, "The Marines need junior officers, Henderson. You've got too much rank."

I can't say that was an easy thing to hear. I did not want to sit by when I felt I could do more, but I had pushed the issue three times. I had to trust that God had other opportunities for me that didn't include active duty.

When I left Camp Lejeune at the end of my active duty tour, I felt unsure as to what lay ahead, but I was heavy with the knowledge that my life was twice bought and paid for, by God eternally and in the present by the men who sacrificed their lives on Iwo Jima that I might return home in one piece. Whether I spoke of Iwo Jima or not, told the tales of those men's lives who were buried on that island, I felt compelled to make sure my life honored their sacrifice. I desired to truly live life to the fullest and to God's glory because to waste my life would be to waste the sacrifices made.

There were also some lessons I had yet to learn about life and about faith. I've heard it said that honor is doing the right thing when no one is looking. When it comes to the Christian journey, honor refers to the quiet places in the heart and soul, the places no one can see but God, and what goes on there.

I was fortunate to start my life with as solid a grounding in the Christian faith as possible. To behave according to the Christian faith wasn't terribly difficult for me - at least in the parts that people could see. I don't want to oversimplify this. I didn't steal or cheat or lie; to do so would simply have been a complete reversal of my character. I was tempted, to be sure, but my father and my father's expectations kept me on the straight and narrow without too much of a struggle. But sin exists in everyone – different sins in different proportions.

Marine basic training, Iwo Jima, and Japan at the end of the war may have seemed a true test of my limits and faith. Certainly, I was pushed to the physical limits, but I don't believe even the grueling 36 days on Iwo Jima tested my faith in the way the day-to-day decisions of the next 60 years would. Because I believed in God before I went to Iwo Jima, God was who I relied on to get me through. I knew surviving was not a result of my skill because I watched Marines who had already survived and done well in previous campaigns in the Pacific Islands die up and down the length of Iwo Jima. And I didn't believe in luck. I had no problem filling in the "Thank _____ I'm alive!" The answer was God every time. Iwo Jima was a lifetime of life and death decisions collapsed into 36 days, but to trust God was instinctual for me. To not cling to my faith would, again, just not be in my character. At the end of the war, I didn't believe God had spared me from death because I was anything special but because He could use me to play some part in His future plan.

When I think about relating the events of the next 60 years of my life, I think that life and faith is key. As faith matures, a Christian may find it easier to control his actions, then easier to control his speech. Last to come is the ability to control thoughts and emotions. All should be completely given over to God. But we can't ever completely stop sinning. There are always those last few hurdles in even the greatest of Christians, some specific sins for that specific individual – pride, lust, jealousy, control. And no matter the sin, it is as black on the soul as if it was murder. No matter how well a believer controls his actions or talk, and no matter how well he minds the rules of faith, sin is still there. We are all sinners.

Trial and temptation came to me over the 60 years after my military service in the gradual accumulation of wealth and success. That accumulation weighed down my soul in the same way an excess of food and a lack of exercise weighs down the body. Soon phrases like "I deserve . . .", "I need to belong to such and such or people will think . . .", "I've earned . . .", and "I can control . . ." became a part of what went through my mind. I wrestled with pride for most of those years. When business deals didn't proceed as planned or a person disappointed me, I sometimes struggled with faith in God. I didn't swear or drink; I treated my family well; I tithed, volunteered, and donated; I worked hard – why didn't everything work the way I thought it should?

On Iwo Jima, there was little time to think. Training and character were the backbone of how one reacted. Life for me over the next 60 years expanded time enough that every decision lost the life and death quality. I knew what I was fighting for in the end – eternal life – but I needed to learn, as every Christian does, the difference between believing in my head that I was saved and living that fact in my very soul. Choosing ethical and moral business partners, focusing on charitable causes, and conducting my-self with honor as a Christian were all important. But none of them exempted me from facing the fact that I was still as black a sinner as the former prison inmates I would seek to rehabilitate. I learned that success is in its own way a trial of faith.

Part II

Civilian Life

Chapter 11

A Civilian's Life

U PON RELEASE FROM ACTIVE DUTY, I returned to my parents' home in Burlington, NC, a man without a clear idea of where he was heading. On a whim, I decided the beach sounded like a fantastic destination to reflect and clear out some of my tangled thoughts. I contacted some of my old college friends. We spent a week or so catching up and relaxing.

It was an odd feeling to stand alone on the beach or to toss a football with a friend while watching the waves and the women—not a care in the world. For the last few years I had moved as part of a group; moments alone, really alone, were hard to come by. As I stood with the beach stretching out miles in either direction, I realized more clearly than I had since leaving the military that my options were now more diverse than simply whether I would live or die that day. I had lived what felt like a lifetime in the last three years, but I was only 24 years old. My choices were as limitless as the beach was long.

Whether or not I could find gainful employment didn't particularly worry me because I had always managed to come up with ways to make money. In college, when finances had been a bit scarce, I developed a variety of schemes to bring in extra money. I worked at a shoe store and helped another student out with his laundry and dry cleaning franchise. We would pick up students' laundry and dry cleaning, transfer it to the actual cleaners, and deliver it back when done. I also bought and sold goods, like neck ties and socks. I purchased socks from hosiery mills located in High Point. The socks had barely discernible flaws. I paid 5 cents for them and sold them for a nice little profit. I also ran what would probably be considered my own little bank, loaning money to other students. I would loan out a dollar and receive two dollars back in a week's time. I did not yet know about usury.

My best plan was the sandwich business I ran my junior year. I had been promoted from cleaning the dormitories my junior and senior year to supervising the program, which often put me in the Student Center. The Student Center was fairly modest in what it offered; it sold snacks and other food items, but the center closed at 8 p.m. and the variety was very limited. Any student not done studying by the time the center closed had to find something to eat downtown. Only a few students had cars; therefore, most had to walk a couple of miles to and from downtown. I decided to run a little sandwich operation with a friend of mine whose family owned a restaurant in New York City. We brought in a big electric grill and sandwich ingredients that didn't require refrigeration. About 9 p.m. we would start grilling sandwiches, and before long we had a booming business. Within a few months, we had several grills operating. It wasn't until the business manager approached me and inquired as to why the electricity had jumped up so dramatically over the last few months that my business partner and I decided to quietly close the sandwich business. Despite those kinds of setbacks, I managed to graduate from college with money in the bank.

With the money I made in college and the money I had saved up from the military, I wasn't desperate for a job. However, idleness was not a preferable state to me. A week at the beach was enough of a break to make me want to start seriously searching for a job.

As I began to cast about for ideas, I received a phone call from a friend of the family in Charlotte, North Carolina.

"Bill, this is Roy Proffit. I heard you're back and ready for work."

"I sure am, sir," I said.

"Why don't you come down to Charlotte, and we can talk about a job opportunity."

I didn't know exactly what he did, but I thought he was in some kind of insurance business. I agreed to come to Charlotte with a fair amount of inward reluctance if he was indeed in the insurance business. I had a fundamental problem with selling someone a product they had to die to use. I'd debated enough in college to know that I was useless in an argument unless I truly believed in what I was defending. That applied to selling as well.

When I arrived, I found out that he was an official for the New York Life Insurance Company, and he wanted me to go though a series of tests to determine my aptitude for the insurance business. I told him I didn't think I was interested. At that time, insurance did not have the various opportunities it has today, and I could not envision managing an insurance agency. I kept asking God if this was where he wanted me; I mean, surely, not in the insurance business, right?

In the end, I agreed to a period of training. When the training period ended, I took a series of tests. They reported that I had a very high aptitude for the insurance business, though I did not know what that meant. I suppose such news could be taken as a compliment. Since I did not have anything else to consider, I took the Burlington territory they offered me. I had been convinced that how you could serve people in the insurance industry, and I took the idea of helping others seriously.

The people involved in the Charlotte office were what we called high rollers, that is they sold large policies to successful professional people. One of their methods of generating business involved inviting prospects to play golf. We played golf several times a week. My main thought at the time was, *Gee, this is a pretty nice way to develop a successful and profitable career.*

After finishing my training in Charlotte and collecting all the collateral materials to open an office, I returned home to Burlington. I began my career by calling on those who had policies with New York Life to see if I could be of service to them and also to generate some prospects. I was not very successful in this effort, so I ran a few ads that did not produce a lot of results either. After several weeks, my father could see that I was not making much progress, so he suggested that I go see an attorney friend of his in Burlington who might be able to steer me in the right direction.

I made an appointment to see this man who was an outstanding citizen in our community. Upon visiting with him, he told me that he would like to take out a policy for his son. I said, "Thank you, God," followed by "Thank you, 'Pepsi'." ("Pepsi" was my nickname for my father. I was fond of nicknames, and ever since my days installing sewer lines at the mill village when my father used to have a cold Pepsi waiting for me after I finished my shift, he'd been "Pepsi" to me.) I suspected this policy was only to encourage me, but nevertheless, I proceeded to negotiate a contract for a $10,000 policy. This was a pretty good size contract for those times, and I left excited because he not only gave me a contract for his son but several potential prospects as well. I made an appointment for his son to get a physical that was required to approve his application.

Other contacts of mine led to contracts, and I started to feel that perhaps insurance was the market for me. I had met a local businessman when I returned from the Marine Corps who worked in a family-owned men's clothing store. Once I had shucked the head-to-toe green uniform, I had to buy a civilian wardrobe; I purchased much of it from his company. We had a lot of mutual interests and soon became good friends. In the course of one of our visits, I discerned that he needed some insurance coverage. He readily agreed to apply for a $5,000 policy.

My confidence soared. These two policies alone would generate a handsome commission. However, a few days later my spirits were dampened when I was informed by the attorney's son that he was entering military service. His application, which contained a war clause, exempted him from being covered and negated any benefit to his policy. The $10,000 contract evaporated. Two days later, I was informed that my friend who had bought the $5,000 policy could not pass the physical. In a matter of a few days, I had lost all the business I had written.

I struggled on for a few days before my bad attitude about the insurance business resurfaced. Once again, I had difficulty being enthusiastic and convincing about a policy a person had to die for in order to make it pay. This was a major stumbling block for my motivation, one I didn't think I could overcome. I called my friend in Charlotte about my decision, and he came to Burlington and had lunch with me, trying to convince me that my experience was not normal, and that I could and would be successful. I finally managed to convince him to the contrary, and we parted ways.

Shortly after my short tenure with life insurance, a friend from my college days, Bob Williams, came by to visit.

"This is a great opportunity Bill. Sears, Roebuck, and Company is opening a large distribution center in Greensboro. They need to hire personnel, and they're going to train them in Atlanta. Give them a call. I've got an interview coming up. You'd be just the guy." He gave me the names and phone number of the official conducting the interviews.

I had liked working in Mr. Yates department store as a youth and thought perhaps Sears, Roebuck and Company would be a good fit. I called and made an appointment to visit them in Greensboro.

The interviewing official, Mr. Ort Jenkins, Jr., told me that Sears, Roebuck does a major part of their business by distributing catalogs that show people what they can order by mail. "We've got distribution centers located here, here, and here," he said, pointing to various locations on the small map on his desk. He took a deep drag off his cigarette, which was making me want one as well. (I'd bet there were few men who left military service without picking up the habit of smoking.) "Each distribution center publishes its own catalog geared towards the buying customs of the customers in that distribution area. Each distribution area is a company within itself, with buyers for various products."

"Is that the position you're considering me for, a buyer?" I asked.

"Yes, that's the one. You said you've had some experience with this before?" he asked.

"Well, more experience in the clothing market in general when I worked in the men's clothing section of a department store, but I'm a quick learner."

"You wouldn't be out there on your own trying to decide what to buy. The home office in Chicago helps the buyers determine the types of merchandise to be sold in that area. You'd be working with, uh, let me check here. Yes, the soft-line. That's clothing, shoes, the like."

I figured I could handle that. Sears had distribution centers in Philadelphia and Atlanta, but nothing in between. A bit of a clean slate. Their market stud-

A Photo Journal

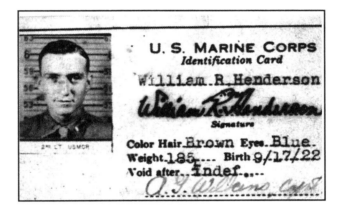

My Father and Mother
Reverend Marion Charles and Ollie Maud Henderson

Wedding Day, Bill and Dot Henderson

Family Photo: Bill, Dot, WH Jr. (Chip) Faithe

Bill and Dot Henderson
50th Wedding Anniversary

Bill Henderson and his
daughter, Faithe

Faithe Giaquuinto,
Husband
Michael, Jessie,
Cassie
and Sydney

Chip and Cindy Henderson
Wedding day

Dot and Bill
Henderson

Bill Henderson
and friend.

Bill and Dot
Henderson

Bill Henderson with
grandaughter
Molly Henderson

U.S.S. Tallabega

P-38 Lightning

PBV Catalina

B-24 - Liberator

Colonel Liversedge

Corporal Stein

Secretary of the Navy
James Forrestal

Tadamichi Kuribayashi

Picture of 1st Flag raised on Mt. Suribachi

The famous flag raising on Iwo Jima

Bill Henderson,Son Chip, William III,
And Nicholas Grandsons on Iwo Jima

Bill Henderson on Iwo Jima

Bill Henderson on Iwo Jima,
Mt. Suribachi in background

ies indicated they could generate a lot more sales if they had a distribution center that could more economically service the Carolinas and Virginia and certain parts of West Virginia and Tennessee. Greensboro had been selected for that distribution center. Land had been purchased, and they were buildinthe center that would open within a year. I thanked Mr. Jenkins for his time, and he told me he would be in touch.

Several days after my interview, I was advised that my application had been approved and that information had been sent on how to report to the Southeastern district office in Atlanta. Bob Williams, who had told me about this opportunity, was also selected, and we made plans to travel to Atlanta together. I felt a new sense of purpose with a job ahead of me, tasks to be done. I liked that the job was more than just any job; there was a bit of a challenge involved with new territory opening up.

While Sears had made arrangements for us to be housed in a hotel and paid all our transportation with an allowance for housing and food, it was only for a limited time. It wasn't long before we set about looking for more permanent housing.

"There's nothing, Bill. I've been looking at advertisements and talking to anyone I can trying to find us a place," Bob complained. "Between the fact that no new construction has been built since the war started and all the G.I.s are coming home, there's pretty close to nothing out there."

We searched for several days without any results. One afternoon, as we left Sears headquarters, we began walking up to a cabaret where we had gone for entertainment and dinner on several occasions.

"What do you think about these places?" I asked, nodding my head at the attractive buildings that made up an apartment complex. "It's only three or four blocks from our office."

Bob laughed. "Sure, why not. What do we have to lose by asking, right? I'll bet there's nothing to be had, but we'll try it anyway."

We went inside and found the manager/owner. Having served in the war probably opened up doors more than anything else.

"Well, seeing as you're both veterans and training with Sears, I'll put you on the waiting list. We'll see what comes along. Housing is pretty hard to come by, that's for sure."

"It sure is, sir," we told him, with our most honest and earnest faces.

We had barely made it to the door, when he called us back.

"It must be your lucky day because I just received notice that a studio apartment has been vacated. We sure appreciate what you boys did in the war, so I'll move you up to the top of the waiting list. There's people ahead of you, but we'll keep that to ourselves, okay?" he said with a wink.

We inspected the apartment and found it to be very attractive and ideal since it was only a short distance to the office and neither one of us owned a car. We had fine restaurants and entertainment facilities within walking distance, and several churches to choose from. It was also within our budget when we put our two allowances together. Most of all, it was available, and at the current time, that in itself was a minor miracle. I said a prayer of thanks to God for bringing the situation together for us. I often found it hard to tell what part God played in the little details of my life, but I had always chosen to thank him regardless because I didn't believe in coincidence.

I met with Mr. Jenkins again, as he had been chosen to be the general manager of the distribution center in Greensboro. He interviewed me to determine what merchandise area was best for me. After a series of tests and a long conversation, he told me I was going to be assigned to train under a man by the name of Charley Burrell. I later found out that Mr. Jenkins and Charley Burrell had started to work with Sears at the same time, and they had an apartment together. I didn't find this out until later, which made me a bit apprehensive.

Charley Burrell was a likeable Canadian and a very competent person. I was fortunate to receive outstanding training. Charley kept me in the dark about my progress in the training program, but he gave me a lot of his work to do without his supervision, which provided me with some confidence that I was doing alright. In fact, I was starting to feel as if Charley had some Col. Liversedge in him – "Henderson, you need this experience."

I went about the business of training and having fun. Bob and I bowled and went to movies, drank beer in some joints, and I spent a fair share of time reading, which was a passion of mine. My parents had purchased a set of the classics when I was young, and books had never been far from my reach. But the fun of reading and movies couldn't take away the fact that I had yet to find a woman – someone I fancied I would like to spend more time with than a few turns on the dance floor. Bob was a great room-mate; however, I wanted more. Then I spied her once while I was returning from a break in the training center's café.

Mr. Jenkins' secretary, Martha Sink Koontz, was standing with a girl whom I thought was the cutest thing I had ever seen. She was like a speckled pup, though maybe she wouldn't have liked that analogy. I stared as I walked by, wondering if she noticed me. That adorable girl occupied my thoughts until I found Martha later and asked who she was. Martha arranged to introduce us, and I finally held her tiny hand in mine and said, "It's my pleasure to meet you, Dorothy Lee Saunders."

"Dot, please call me Dot. And it's a pleasure to meet you," she said with a smile.

I wasted little time before I asked her out. She was from Reidsville, NC, and working as a secretary. I listened to the sound of her voice as much as her words. There was something different about her. To say I knew I would marry her right off would be overstating it, but deep inside I think I felt that God had found me a wife. That first night we double-dated with friends, we talked and laughed. At 6'2", I towered over her a bit as we walked to the movies; she was so petite. I don't remember the movie, but I remember it was a romance-type film, the type the ladies melt over. My friend and I laughed and joked our way through it, and our dates were a bit upset.

"Bill, you've taken all the enjoyment out of it," she complained to me afterward, gently rapping her gloved hand on my forearm as punishment.

"You have to admit it was rather silly, Dot. Come on, it was rather over the top, don't you think?"

"Well, maybe," she conceded, still looking at me half-seriously as if I'd ruined the evening. "You'll have to make it up to me, you know. Another movie, and this time you sit and enjoy it. I won't hear you say otherwise."

"Another movie it is then," I agreed, ready to accept such a punishment.

Dot and I shared an intense affection for each other, and together with a group of our young friends we made the rounds of clubs and restaurants, enjoying our youth and freedom. Before too long, I started to seek out Dot's company alone. On one of the first occasions that we planned to go to a movie alone, we arrived at the theater a little late for the first evening show. Not wanting to go in to a movie that was partially over, we decided to stop for coffee and dessert at a restaurant across the street. As we stepped into the restaurant, Dot confessed that in rushing to get ready, she had not eaten anything and was quite hungry.

"I'm quite famished," she said, as I watched her pull her white gloves from her hands with a pull on each fingertip before she tugged the whole thing off. I watched as she extracted her hand from the other glove and carefully placed them in her purse.

"Hungry? Well then, you must eat something more than dessert. I can't have your stomach making all sorts of noises through the movie or have you fainting at the ticket booth. You'll just have to order dinner," I insisted quite firmly.

Dot ordered her dinner from the waiter, as I started to look over the menu. Being of limited resources at the time, it suddenly struck me that it was quite possible I didn't have enough money on me for dinner and a movie.

"Dot, if you'll excuse me for a moment. I need to visit the men's room." "Sir," the waiter said, "would you like to order?"

"I'll just be a minute," I told him and made my way to the men's room.

A quick count of all the money I had on me revealed that if I wanted to avoid embarrassment, I could afford a cup of coffee and a sandwich and still have enough to cover Dot's dinner, the movie, and transportation home. I ordered my cheese sandwich, weakly apologizing for not ordering a full dinner, although I also was hungry. The cheese sandwich was about 35 cents, and I had just enough money to leave a modest tip.

I looked at my future wife that night and had the first of many revelations that would be key to our marital success. In this case, my revelation was to always make sure to have sufficient finances when taking Dot out to dinner. I like to eat, but Dot likes to dine.

Chapter 12

The Married Life

MY TRAINING WITH SEARS WAS THE back drop to my relationship with Dot. I would work hard regardless of the situation, but the fact that I thought I might ask Dot to marry me added a new dimension to how I viewed my job. I routinely met with Mr. Jenkins to review my progress. The first of these meetings had me more nervous than usual, because, as I said, Charley Burrell hadn't provided me with much feedback and was continually adding responsibility. I was hoping that fact was a positive sign, but I wasn't sure. In the military, having to report to the commander was a bad sign since, more often than not, something had gone wrong and someone needed a reprimanding.

With a fair amount of apprehension, I reported to Mr. Jenkins and tried to forget the kind of concern I felt when I reported to the Commanding General of Camp LeJeune.

"Have a seat, Bill," said Mr. Jenkins.

I sat, stiffly. I found myself talking in my head, answering any complaints or issues, before I realized that Mr. Jenkins was telling me everything was proceeding quite well.

"We'll be sending you to Greensboro as a buyer for the women's shoe department," Mr. Jenkins was saying. I now had a destination and a timeline. What I wanted was a wife to accompany me.

On New Year's Eve, 1946, Dot and I made our way to a party in Greensboro, NC, in a convertible with John Armfield, a friend of mine. As the clock struck midnight, I slipped a ring from my pocket and asked Dot, "Do you think you could tolerate me for the rest of your life?" Dot decided that she could and agreed to marry me. I looked down at the tiny slip of a woman she was and thanked God for such a wonderful gift.

I had grown up watching my mother and father model a solid Christian marriage, and I never doubted from childhood that I would want such a marriage in my life. My parents were not overly demonstrative, but their love and affection was apparent in the way they talked to each other and cared for each other. My father talked to my mother with love and respect, touched her gently on her shoulder at times, and looked at her in such a way that I could see he would be crushed if something happened to her. For my mother's part, I could see her care and concern in the way she packed a meal for my father, fussed over him before he went out the door, and worried over his return should the evenings turn late. She took his change in career in stride and worked as a partner, creating a peaceful home despite the constant moves. They were a team, it seemed to me, and that was what I wanted, although my understanding of what that meant and how it was achieved was still rather naïve at that point.

Dot planned for our wedding to take place at her home church in Reidsville. I was happy to leave all the details to her as I continued my training for Sears. We had agreed on a date for the wedding so it would coincide with the completion of my training and our move to Greensboro. Six weeks before the wedding, I almost lost Dot to an emergency appendectomy.

She lay on the hospital bed post-surgery, white as the sheets, and worked up over how to handle the wedding.

"What should we do, Bill? We'll have to postpone the wedding and be married in Greensboro. I don't want to wait though, do you?"

I held her cool hand in mine, running my fingers lightly over the skin on the topside of her hand. "No, Dot, I don't want to wait either. Why don't we see what we can arrange on this end before we move.

Let mefigure something out." *Poor thing*, I thought. *She's normally a whirl of activity and efficiency. And here she lies, unable to re-plan one of the biggest events of her life.*

Frankly, I couldn't imagine waiting now to marry her. There's nothing like a death scare to make one quickly move ahead. It was funny how I knew in my heart that God controlled all our lives and there was nothing in this world that would compare to the joy we would feel in heaven, but how I desperately still wanted to feel the joy of marriage and a wife before I died.

Dot recovered quickly, as I knew she would. She was tiny, but she had a formidable will. She managed to arrange for a wedding ceremony in the chapel at Emory University on March 15, 1947. The change of date and location was difficult for our families, but they were happy to attend considering the circumstances. My father performed the marriage ceremony. There was one part of the ceremony, though, we laugh about even now.

"Dorothy Lee Saunders," my father solemnly said, "do you take this man to be your lawful wedded husband, in sickness and in health," – and then came the slip – "poor or poorer, 'til death do you part?" My eyebrows went up and our eyes met.

"I do," she said, not knowing how prophetic my father's slip would be.

My roommate in our little efficiency apartment was kind enough to move in with some other friends for a couple of weeks until we moved to Greensboro. The Alumni Office at Emory University requested permission to film our wedding, which has allowed us to relive the moment and enjoy the memories and not a few laughs over my father's mistake.

Chapter 13

Greensboro: Risks and Rewards

G REENSBORO PRESENTED THE SAME set of challenges for those in search of accommodations as Atlanta had. The local military base had been a staging area for military personnel being deployed overseas, which meant there were a lot of military families living in the area. With the construction only now restarting, there was little to be found in the way of housing. We reserved a room in a private home where we stayed only two or three nights because, once again, God provided what we needed.

Shortly after our wedding was announced in the Greensboro paper, a Mrs. Lewis called Dot. Mrs. Lewis introduced herself as being a former resident of Reidsville who now lived in Greensboro. She said, "I presume you'll be looking for a place to live, and being as our home is only two or three blocks from where you and Bill will be working, well, we'd be delighted to have you consider renting a room in our home. Why, we have just the bedroom suite for you, and the home's quite well appointed, if I say so myself."

Dot assured her, "We would be ever so grateful with housing so hard to come by. I am sure your home will be perfect."

The Lewis's were a Godsend, not only because they offered us a room but because they taught us some of the basics of running a home and managing finances. Living there was a short course in household management.

We had the privacy of our own suite, and the Lewis's rearranged their eating schedule by eating breakfast at mid-morning and their evening meal in mid-afternoon. During evenings and weekends, Mr. Lewis, who was in the financial consulting business and semi-retired, discussed finances with me while Mrs. Lewis, who was an excellent cook and household manager, taught Dot how to cook and plan meals. Dot had never really cooked that much – she grew up on a farm where they had tenants who not only worked on the farm but helped with the housework, including preparation of the food and cleaning. About the only thing Dot could cook when we married were cakes. Mrs. Lewis taught her how to prepare menus and shop for food, what portions of meat were best, and the like. Living with them was also a blessing because we did not own a car, and we could walk the few blocks to work.

The time finally came when we felt that we were imposing on Mr. and Mrs. Lewis because they constantly had to adjust to our rather busy schedules, so we moved into an apartment in a huge old house in downtown Greensboro. Mrs. Hutton, whose husband had been an outstanding attorney in Greensboro and was deceased, owned the house. It was her family's home, a beautiful old house but in need of a lot of repairs.

"Did you run into Mrs. Hutton again?" Dot asked me as I closed the door to our apartment and leaned down to kiss her on the cheek.

"Did I ever. That poor old woman. She cornered me down by the stairs. It must have been 15 minutes Dot, and I'm still not sure what she was really telling me. I kept trying to start up the stairs. As soon as I would take a step, she would start talking again. I never thought I'd make it up here. Although now that I'm up here, I can tell the heat still hasn't made it up." Mrs. Hutton was an unusual lady, somewhat distracted and removed, lonely beyond bearing. She wandered around the house in her nightgown without regard for her personal appearance. For our part, we overlooked her disheveled state and listened as best we could, but I have to admit we unkindly referred to our accommodations as the Hutton Nuthouse.

Our apartment was in a fourth floor garret, and unfortunately the heat had a hard time reaching us. After a number of months living in constant cold, Martha Sink Koontz, who had introduced me to my wife, told Dot about a housing situation that sounded very interesting. A family friend's husband had died, and she was going to go to Florida for a year to see if she wanted to move there. She wanted someone to move in and look after her house while she was gone. Martha introduced us to the lady. After interviewing us, she called to say that she would be glad for us to move in and suggested a very modest rental. She lived in a nice home in the Irvin Park section of Greensboro. In fact, we had four bedrooms. Dot suggested that we consider renting one of the bedrooms to some of our acquaintances at Sears who did not have satisfactory housing. It seemed a good opportunity to share our good fortune with our friends. Also, with the rent they paid us, we were living in the house with little expense.

As the only young couple among our acquaintances at Sears with such spacious accommodations, we opened up our home to all of our friends. Almost every evening, couples would drop by. In fact, we almost had a 24/7 party.

My training at Sears ended with orders from the company's headquarters in Chicago and our move to Greensboro, NC. Under Mr. Burrell's supervision, we selected the merchandise that would be distributed through the Greensboro area catalog. One of the benefits of the constant flow of young women and men through our home was it gave me ample opportunity to keep an eye on the fashions. I found myself looking at women's feet more frequently than ever before. The buyers in the home office in Chicago had basically selected the various styles; however, we had the opportunity to review their decisions and give our input since we were more familiar with the potential market.

Catalogs had been distributed from the Philadelphia and Atlanta offices to portions of this area, and they had sales records that indicated to some extent what volume of business could be expected. This had to be adjusted to the fact that there was a pent-up demand because of the shortage of merchandise during the war years. Upon reviewing the styles and quantities, I approved the styles but felt they had underestimated the volume of sales that could be generated out of the Greensboro area. Sears had such a fine reputation in this market area, and I thought the increased service that customers could anticipate would generate a lot more business than the home office in Chicago had projected. I talked to my merchandise supervisor and ultimately to Mr. Jenkins, asking permission to increase the quantities substantially.

The fact that my supervisors agreed to let me increase the projected sales volume was a vote of confidence in my ability, and I did not take it lightly. I was a fairly serious-minded business person. That's not to say I didn't love to have fun like any other young man my age, but I particularly enjoyed the challenges and risks involved in business transactions.

In the end, I increased the sales projection by approximately 20% across the board. The amount of inventory is a very critical factor in the mercantile business. If the company carries too much inventory of a particular item, it has a lot of money invested. When the inventory does not sell, the company has to sell it at a severe discount, resulting in substantial loss. On the other hand, if there is not enough inventory to cover sales, then the company loses the benefits of advertising and promoting sales activities. Not only that, but if the company cannot fill the orders of customers, the customers lose confidence and are reluctant to order merchandise in the future. Deciding where to set sales projections and how much to order was not a simple task. There could be serious consequences for making the wrong choices.

We had anywhere from 90 to 125 different styles in each of the main catalogs. Which styles to have in inventory was only one decision that had to be made though. Were there more women in the area with wide feet, narrow feet, size 5, size 9, fond of red or fond of blue? Would they prefer the shoes with the tiny bows or the ones with the polka dots? I committed our distribution center to a substantial inventory with an investment of thousands upon thousands of dollars. I don't think the merchandise manager or the general manager ever realized how much I had over-bought, except that when the inventory began to accumulate, the merchandise manager became a bit concerned. There were days I went home that I felt a bit of the concern as well, but I didn't share that with Dot. I didn't want to cause her worry. My only choice seemed to remain steadfastly optimistic because the alternative was beyond me.

I can only say the Lord must have become very interested in my moving those shoes because my next evaluation was as outstanding as it was unbelievable. A buyer's evaluation was based on how profitably their department performed. If there was too much inventory, it adversely affected profitability. Too little inventory meant lost sales and a cost per sale increase. Therefore, buying the right style, the right number of widths and sizes, etc., was critical to profitability. Any order that couldn't be filled was classified as an omission. In all of Sears' history, my department had never had one day that they did not omit some orders. My inventory was so substantial that I didn't omit an order for the life of our first catalog, approximately 90 to 120 days.

When I chose such an abundance of inventory, I ran the risk that I would end up with a rather full distribution center of unsold shoes at the end of the catalog season. I truly believe the hand of God intervened because the buyers in the other distribution centers had been conservative with Chicago's approval in anticipating the business. They were all short of inventory, and I, of course, was fat with it. All the buyers communicated daily among themselves, so I was aware of the shortages and was able to slough off my excess inventory to those buyers who had under-bought. This not only took care of my surplus inventory but engendered a feeling of good will between me and those buyers I was able to help out.

I ended up at the end of the catalog season with the lowest amount of inventory according to my volume of any department throughout the Sears Roebuck mail order division. Also, I set a record for not having an omission during this entire period. I looked a whole lot smarter than I was when Mr. Jenkins called me into his office.

"Bill, come on in. Sit down, sit down," he said, motioning to the chair in front of his desk. "Quite a first run you've had with this catalog. You've done well, very well."

"Thank you, sir. I suppose it was the training."

"Well, don't be so modest now." If I had been next to him, I think he would've been slapping me on the back the whole time. "I've been asked to offer you a promotion to the home office in Chicago. I can't tell you how many times they checked that there hadn't been some error, something they had overlooked. But, no mistake. You made it through the whole catalog season without an omission.

That's pretty darn remarkable."

"Mr. Jenkins, I'm quite flattered." I did not add that I surely knew my good fortune was not due to my expertise. "I'd like to discuss this with my wife, if I could have the time to do so."

The Private Sector

A FTER DISCUSSING THE OPPORTUNITY with Dot and prayerfully considering it, we decided to decline. I had planned to be with Sears long enough to get grounded in the retail business because I had always planned to be in business for myself and accordingly had been making some plans. In some military publication, I read about an air force base somewhere in the western part of the United States that had provided laundry service for the base personnel. Some manufacturing company had modified automatic washing machines and dryers, which enabled them to be operated by depositing coins. Since most of the manufacturing of equipment for civilians had been suspended during the war, most families did not have automatic washing machines or dryers.

The air force base, recognizing this problem, had solved it by opening a self-service laundry on the base. As I reflected on this, I thought this might be a good business opportunity, since civilians were experiencing the same shortage of washing machines and dryers.

My brother, M.C. Jr., had just been released from active duty in the Air Force. He had been on duty in Europe and had returned home prepared to re-enter civilian life. I discussed the idea with him, and we decided to open a self-service laundry, similar to what the Air Force had done.

Washing machines and dryers were not available through regular appliance stores. M.C. made a contact with a wholesale distributor in the Philadelphia, PA, area and negotiated to buy 20 coin-operated washing machines and a couple of large dryers. We bought a piece of land in Burlington, NC, and built a building. M.C. supervised and assisted in installing the equipment.

The business was very successful, but that accounted for only part of the positive feelings I derived from the business. We were filling a very real need in the community. On Saturdays, I traveled from Greensboro to the laundry to assist because Saturday was the busiest day of the week and M.C. could use the extra help. For the most part, though, I was an investor in the laundry; M.C. handled all the day-to-day operations.

After several months of operation, ten of the washing machines began to break down. My brother had a mechanical aptitude, but he could not keep them in operation. Unfortunately, because M.C. had bought them through an irregular source, there was no manufacturer's warranty. The ten machines were not a very popular brand, so he looked about for better machines. He was able to find ten new machines of first-line quality to replace them, but it meant we would have to spend $4,000.

I had invested all of my savings when we paid cash for the original machines, the land, and the building. M.C. had the money for his half, but I needed $2,000 to pay for my half of the new machines. I grew up during the Great Depression era and learned during that time what could happen to people who borrowed money. When the down-turn in the economy occurred, those who had borrowed money did not have the resources to repay their loans. Many people lost their land, their farms, their businesses, their homes – virtually everything they owned because the lending institutions foreclosed on their property. It was ingrained in me to see borrowing money as bad. Unfortunately, I had no other option.

I went to the bank with some degree of apprehension because I had never dealt with a bank under these circumstances. I had only used the bank for a checking account and to save my money. Imagine my surprise to find out I had considerable collateral. When I requested a loan of $2,000, the bank readily agreed. I agreed to repay the note over 12 months. I figured that between myself and Dot, our income was about $375 per month. I didn't realize that my payments would be $200/month, which would leave us $175 a month for all of our living expenses.

Dot responded to my news of the loan admirably by adjusting our budget so that we met all of our expenses on time. I realized daily over that year, with our budget so tight that we restricted ourselves to spending only $5 on each other for Christmas. What a true gift my wife was. During that year, we became familiar with all 57 varieties of Heinz soups, and our movie attendance was restricted to once a month. Not once did Dot complain or fail to find a way to make the money stretch. When Christmas came around, Dot was very faithful and I received a hand-painted necktie for Christmas. I had sneaked aside a little extra money and bought her a beautiful pair of lounging pajamas and a matching robe, which she received with mixed emotions. I knew she appreciated the gift, all the more because she knew I had to have used money set aside for my refreshments during break time to add to the $5 we had allocated. The smile on her face was worth whatever I had sacrificed.

The Lord blessed our business beyond what we could have imagined. With the self-service laundry in Burlington doing so well, we opened one in High Point. I decided to move to Reidsville and open a self-service laundry there as well. I located a building in an excellent location on Main Street in Reidsville. I bought the equipment through a local furniture and appliance store and supervised the installation.

My plans went off without a hitch except for our sign. I painted the building myself, inside and out, and made plans for our opening. The building was located at the beginning of a curve in the street, with a large blank wall next to the street, which seemed to me an excellent place to have our sign. We had named the self-service laundries "U Wash It." I hired a sign painter to paint the name on the side of the building. This sign painter sketched out his letters and began painting the sign from back to front. He started by painting the T, then the I, then H, then S; it began raining, so he left, saying he would be back to finish it after it stopped raining.

Eager to see how the lettering looked so far, I ventured out in the rain to take a look. I almost went into shock when I looked at the four letters he had painted. They were almost two feet tall! I could imagine somebody reporting this incident to the local newspaper. I called the painter and told him to get back immediately and cover up what he had done. By the time he arrived, it had stopped raining, so he finished. No one ever mentioned the sign to me. I don't know if traffic stopped during the rain or if people didn't look, but nevertheless, I was grateful not to have to suffer that embarrassment.

My wife kept the home running while I worked the six days a week our laundry was open. I would open at 8 o'clock in the morning and stay open until 8 at night. With an hour of clean up after closing, I rarely made it home before 9 p.m. Fortunately, we found an apartment about a mile from the business, and I was able to walk to and from work. We still had not bought an automobile because I didn't want to borrow money, and I had utilized all of my savings to invest in the laundry.Another laundry opened in Reidsville, and again we felt the Lord had protected us. I cannot explain how I knew it, but I did. I know my success could not possibly be simple luck or any business savvy I had. With each bit of fortune, Dot and I were quick to thank the providence of God; we prayed together often for God's guidance in all we did. In those early days of our marriage, God blessed us with plenty of ideas and successes, and we in turn invested what time and money we had back into the community and in the church.

With the competing laundry, we were blessed with the better location and the fortune of having an employee who had a lot of friends. Our business was a little more profitable than our competition's, but less than I anticipated. I started to look around for another opportunity that would meet a community need and use up the extra space I had at the laundry. I decided to open a remnant shop.

I would buy at the end of the season surplus merchandise from cloth manufacturers and distributors, at a discounted price, and package them into pieces sufficient in size to make dresses, shorts, or some other apparel. Buying them at such a discount, I was able to sell them at about half the price they would normally pay at a retail establishment. I bought a considerable amount from Sears because, as I stated earlier, at the end of a catalog season any merchandise not sold would be sold at a severe discount, which again permitted me to sell the remnants at a very attractive price.

I continued to develop businesses over the next few years, either by myself or with partners. The first was an Economy Department Store that I opened with a partner. We sold everything from clothing to furniture - items I had picked up for ten to twenty-five cents on the dollar. This venture was very profitable with a substantial clientele. After a few years, my partner, who I had trained, was managing the store and decided he would like to own it. I sold it and moved on to my next venture in men's clothing.

I didn't spend a lot of time praying for God to bring business ideas to mind. I believed that if I did my part - considered ethical business opportunities that served a need – God would direct my path. My parents used to read to us the parable of the servants and the talents from the book of Luke: "To those who use well what they are given, even more will be given. But from those who are unfaithful, even what little they have will be taken away." While I believed myself to be a fairly ordinary young man, I enjoyed putting together business deals and making a company grow, especially if it helped people. To not use those talents, in my mind, would have been to waste what God have given me, no matter how small. I found that being in business simply for the sake of making money didn't appeal to me nearly as much as making a difference with whatever business venture I started. There is much to be said, though, for making "clean" money that can be used for greater purposes.

Such was my mindset when I cast about for business ideas. When I sold the Economy Department Store, I became intrigued by a friend's family business, which was tailor-made clothing. After working in Belk's during my youth, I was aware that many men could not be properly fit with off-the-rack clothing. I spent time studying my friend's business. I must admit that I had a certain passion for men's clothing, so the idea of opening a store that sold made-to-measure menswear with a variety of wonderful fabrics to choose from really interested me. The prices were not a great deal higher than what was already being paid for clothes that didn't fit or had to be drastically altered, and I would not have to carry a large inventory, which reduced the overhead.

In 1951, I opened an exclusive men's store called Rockingham Clothiers with one hundred to one hundred and fifty samples of cloth. These samples were provided by the company who did the actual tailoring. Because of the personal attention required in this business and my interest, I spent most of my time operating this store. The lady who had been my assistant helper managed the U Wash It Laundry and remnant shop. Not too long after Rockingham Clothiers began to prosper, I had an offer from a local business man to purchase the U Wash It Laundry. I sold the laundry and chose to focus on Rockingham Clothiers, while my brother continued to manage the laundries we had in Burlington and High Point.

My brother, who also had an entrepreneurial spirit, convinced me during this time to partner with him in buying a poultry processing plant in High Point, NC. This was one of the few business ventures that I realized in hindsight I could've left to someone else. For anyone who has ever been in a chicken processing plant, the reasons are obvious. Chicken processing is a dirty, hard, and unpleasant business. The chickens are put in scalding water and the insides ripped out. Processing chickens was along the lines of picking cotton for me – if I didn't have to do it for my livelihood, I had just as soon not. My parents seemed to feel the same, and they continually urged me to find a different job for M.C.

I believed that God was rewarding my diligence and hard work by sending more opportunities my way. During this time, I was approached by the owners of an exclusive men's store in Reidsville and offered a partnership in the business. The business was started in 1875 and had been in the same family for over 75 years. However, the men in the family had died out, and the husband of one of the heirs was operating the business. Frankly, he did not know what he was doing because he had spent his lifetime in the tobacco business. He, along with another man who was involved in the tobacco business, had bought the family's interest and while they had the intelligence and the money to operate the business, they could not compete with a nearby men's store that was owned and operated by two very popular, energetic young men who were experienced in the clothing business. They said if I would come and join them and manage the business they would give me a 1/3 interest. Although Rockingham Clothiers was growing, this would present me with an opportunity of greater import. I accepted their offer and took over the management of Williams and Company.

I remodeled the store, eliminated out-of-style and out-of-date merchandise, and re-stocked it with contemporary clothing. Fortunately, since Williams and Company had been in business for so long, they had the franchise for excellent brand name manufacturers. The business was growing, but much of the profit in Williams and Company was still generated by the made-to-measure portion of the business. When I became manager, the former partner who had been managing quit, so I was the only active partner. After a year or so, I realized that the silent partners did not contribute anything and I did not need their capital anymore. So I bought their interest.

My brother, who was operating the poultry processing plant and supervising the laundries in Burlington and High Point, became stressed out because of the time required for him to fulfill his obligations. He had always been interested in the clothing business, so when one of the suppliers whom I bought merchandise from advised me that the owners of an old, well-established men's store in Mount Airy, NC had died and the family was interested in selling the business, I immediately contacted them. After several weeks of negotiation, my brother and I bought the store. He moved to Mount Airy. Owning two stores increased our efficiency and improved our buying power. We also could switch merchandise from one store to another, which enabled us to capture business we would otherwise lose. These two businesses proved to be very profitable for us, as most of the businesses had that I became involved in.

Chapter 15

The Prisoners

BY 1952, I HAD BECOME VERY IN volved in the Junior Chamber of Commerce (Jaycees), first in Reidsville at the local level, and later as a District Vice President, and finally President of the North Carolina chapter. I received satisfaction from this position because it allowed me to develop and direct programs I believed could have the greatest impact. We worked on a program to grow the membership, and then one to increase voter turnout in regional and national elections. But the program that meant the most to me was the prisoner rehabilitation program.

As I've mentioned, when I was growing up, we came into contact with people from different races and economic levels. We helped people first and foremost because God commanded it and because we believed that each person had been created in the image of God. God would judge how we treated society's most insignificant individuals. I had always felt that if I kept my mind and energies focused on the welfare of others, my welfare would be taken care of. It was out of these beliefs that I turned my attention to the prisoners of North Carolina.

At the time, North Carolina's prisoner recidivism rate was high, around 65%. In the mid-1950's, racism was rampant, and the black population in the prisons was disproportionately large in comparison to the general population. Few people cared about helping former prisoners find their way once released, and even fewer cared for the bulk of those released because the prisoners were black.

I visited several prisons. A sense of hopelessness dogged the prisoners, on the inside as well as once they were released. Having served time for their crimes, they served time again on the outside, marked by their experience any time they had to explain where they had been. As a Christian, I could identify with the idea of being defined by my sins and unable to find my way out. I believed that what these men needed was to know that someone cared, that someone was invested in helping them find meaning in a productive life and value in them as persons. Otherwise the only place they will feel they belong will be in prison or on the outside once again amongst criminals.

With the approval and assistance of the North Carolina Department of Prisons, we developed a system of interviews to qualify prisoners for the program. Prisoners were provided with job training while still in prison, and members from the Jaycees would pick them up from prison, help them find a job, provide emotional support, and aid them in becoming involved in church and the community. We were anchors to keep them in the world outside of prison. The program didn't always work, but for those former inmates that it did work, we could see the hopelessness drain from their eyes over time as they realized that someone, some one person at least, cared what they did and whether or not they existed. That was surely the hope I found daily in Christ, that no matter how insignificant my one life might be, it mattered enough to God to send His Son to redeem it.

Chapter 16

On the Home Front

OVER THOSE FIRST TEN YEARS OR SO
after Dot and I married, when I
was growing my businesses and becoming involved in community and
civic affairs, I had little time to grow
my marriage. Dot worked a bit initially, but by the time we moved into
our first home, she was managing all
the household affairs and no longer
working outside the home. I often felt
aware in the late hours of the day,
when I would return home to my dinner being kept warm or Dot holding
off on eating so that we could eat together, of how fortunate I was in the
woman God had led to be my wife.
Dot never complained about my hours,
even though I was involved in several
businesses, continued to serve in the
Marine Corps Reserves, and worked
an ever-increasing number of hours

with the Jaycees and other service organizations. She never led me to believe she was unhappy or lacking, and she managed our home and finances better than I could have hoped for. We both found pleasure in church and community activities.

My youth and naiveté allowed me to accept Dot's silence as confirmation of her happiness, so I didn't ask if there was anything more she might need from me or if our life was what she had envisioned for herself. It was not as though I mistreated her; I simply did not take her into account in the grand scheme of my decisions except to say that when I made business decisions it was to help secure her financial future as well as mine and that I tried to be the head of our Christian home through prayer and being involved in our church and community.

I continued in this manner, lulled by business successes and a quiet home front, so that I rarely asked myself the hard, introspective questions that might have deepened my faith earlier on. I had always had a strong faith, but faith is a journey, no matter what point one starts at. My faith had always been strong, but in small degrees I was failing as a husband to be one with my wife, and I was beginning to enjoy my success in such a way that I had grown comfortable in my surroundings and could not imagine that they should change for any good reason. I found myself wanting things and expecting to receive them. I was fond of saying that I could endure almost anything, but living in a trailer home was not one of them.

One day, eight years into our marriage, I found myself rushing once again to the hospital to be by Dot's side. Only a few weeks had passed since Dot had shared the happy news with me that we were to be parents. I remember that day because it was as if a whole new world had opened up, a new venture. My father had been a good example of a Christian man, but he hadn't had much spare time for his children because he was busy ministering to the members of his church. I wanted to be different for my children; I wanted them to know I was there for them.

I reached the hospital to find Dot pale but coping. She nearly died from a tubular pregnancy. I held her hand as I sat next to her. I have always found women indecipherable, and I confess that I'm not sure of everything that went through Dot's mind that day. We did not openly confess every feeling and thought to each other. But we prayed together over our loss of a child and God's favor in Dot's healing and recovery. We prayed together that while we didn't know God's will that we would joyfully accept it nonetheless.

I began to look at Dot differently, or rather at my connection to her differently. Of all relationships that God blesses us with, marriage is the most special, the closest opportunity we have to show and share in the kind of love that God has gifted us with. As I felt Dot's soft skin between my hands, saw the con-cern, sadness, and fatigue in her face, I wondered what she thought of me as a husband. I realized with clarity that I had for the most part dragged her along through the last eight or so years, proceeding through my life with her as more of an assistant than a partner. When I was in training and in combat, I didn't need to know exactly what the other Marines were doing, but I needed to know that we were all focused on a common mission and purpose. I had assumed that Dot was joined with me in the purpose at hand though I gave her little opportunity to pro-vide input on the path we had chosen. I knew she had little interest in the details of my business inter-ests, and while I didn't bore her with those, I also didn't ask her to sign on for any particular course of action in our marriage and life – I took her agree-ment for granted.

I silently prayed to God that He would bless me with the ability to lead in our marriage but not to dictate. I wanted a partner in my marriage; I wanted Dot to be truly joyful, even when life seemed to be falling apart, because joy meant we were at peace with each other and accepting of God's will with a thankful heart. To feel joyful in the midst of resent-ment would be a hard place to reach, and even though I had no indication from Dot that she was resentful, I knew I would be if I were her.

"Dot, we'll try again for a baby when you're better. Don't worry. We'll try again," I kept my hands around hers, not wanting to let go.

And each time I thought that we would try again, inside I was thinking too that I would try, I would try again to be the husband I knew God wanted and that Dot deserved.

On April 10, 1955, God blessed us with our first child, a daughter. "Let's name her Faithe, Dot, because that's what it took for her to be born." Faithe was followed by her brother William, Jr. (Chip) on May 16, 1957, and our little family was complete.

Do not merely listen to the word, and so deceive yourselves. Do what it says. Anyone who listens to the word but does not do what it says is like a man who looks at his face in a mirror and, after looking at himself, goes away and immediately forgets what he looks like. But the man who looks intently into the perfect law that gives freedom, and continues to do this, nor forgetting what he has heard, but doing it – he will be blessed in what he does.

James 1:22-25

Chapter 17

North Carolina Politics

I HAD CONSIDERED POLITICS A PART OF my future. Being involved in business brought me into contact with a number of politicians over the years, and my feeling had always been that choosing a political life meant selling a part of one's soul. The business of politics involved becoming beholden to one set of contacts or another, or paying back investors and backers through side deals or special favors. I thought no one came to politics without a lot of strings attached.

When I was elected President of the North Carolina Junior Chamber of Commerce, I found myself in the company of politicians at every turn. One of my main responsibilities as president was to visit the 250 or so clubs throughout North Carolina and be available to speak at the various events they sponsored. Finding it difficult to manage Williams and Company and travel as much as I needed to, I brought on a partner who took over the management duties so that I could focus on the Jaycees more fully.

It was during my travels throughout North Carolina when I met a man whom I believed to be one of the few truly honest politicians. Luther Hodges had been President of Fieldcrest Mills, a division of Marshall Fields, when he announced his candidacy for Lieutenant Governor for the State of North Carolina. He approached me about supporting him, and I agreed to do so. I knew him as an intelligent man of integrity who had not been involved in politics; therefore could bring a fresh, business-like approach to North Carolina government without the traditional strings attached from years of political service. Mr. Hodges ran a very vigorous and successful campaign and was elected Lt. Governor. Mr. William Umstead was elected Governor, but, unfortunately, Mr. Umstead died shortly after he became Governor and Mr. Hodges was elevated to serve as Governor for the rest of Umstead's term.

Mr. Hodges' home was about 14 miles from Reidsville in a town called Eden, which was then three separate communities: Leaksville, Spray, and Draper. Although he spent his working days in Raleigh, he would frequently go back to Eden for the weekend. During the Christmas and New Year's holiday, Governor Hodges had a reception at his home, and Dot and I were invited. Since Dot was not feeling well, I attended alone. That party was the beginning of my political career.

At the party, I struck up a conversation with Paul Johnson, a man I had met during the Hodges' campaign. Paul Johnson was a very competent and intelligent individual. Upon graduating from the University of North Carolina at Chapel Hill, where he had been editor of the Law Review, Paul found employment with the Institute of Government, an organization whose aim was to create a center for educating politicians. At the moment, he was Mr. Hodges administrative assistant.

"Bill," he said, looking at me over the rim of his glass as he raised it in my direction and took a drink, "you better come down to Raleigh and join us. I think we're doing some good. I guarantee you, it's challenging and interesting. I think you'd like it."

He had no idea that I had already declined the offer. Governor Hodges, who was standing nearby, overheard Paul and remarked to Paul, but I'm sure as much if not more so to me, "Don't ask him anymore. I've asked him several times and he is just like all these other businessmen – they complain and complain about government, and when you give them the opportunity to do something about it, and they won't do a thing."

I turned him off, until I was driving home that evening and I couldn't stop Governor Hodges' comment from playing over and over again in my head.

I reflected on what he said and quickly resolved that he was absolutely right. I had no desire to move to Raleigh and be involved in state government. I was doing well in my business and didn't want to interrupt the plans I had. But I felt something, as if God had placed this challenge before me, to make a difference and to be an example, an honest public servant.

Over the next few days, I talked it over with Dot. I was working hard at trying to include her more fully in decisions. While these discussions usually ended with Dot saying, "Bill, if you think it's something you need to do . . ." or "Bill, if you think it's something God is leading you to, then you need to do it. I will support you however I can." Together we decided to consider being a part of Governor Hodges' administration. I say "consider" because I realized I was not so wholeheartedly given over to joining the political ranks that I was willing to do just any job.

I called up Governor Hodges. "Governor, this is Bill Henderson. I've spent some time thinking about your comment at the party. I'd like to come talk with you about joining your administration when my term as the Jaycee president is up."

Governor Hodges for his part showed little surprise at my decision. He thanked me for taking the time to consider it thoughtfully and told me he looked forward to the end of my term when we could talk. I turned complete management of Williams and Company over to my partner, and in May I traveled to Raleigh to see Governor Hodges.

I was ushered into Governor Hodges office, a wood-paneled, well-appointed room that felt comfortable and yet serious. "I'm ready to work, Governor. What did you have in mind for me?" I was quite curious as to where Governor Hodges would use me, and I had some ideas of my own too, places where I might prove valuable and resourceful.

"Good to see you here, Bill, finally. The first thing I want you to do is go to the Prison Department."

I have to admit my heart fell a bit at those words. I immediately thought he was referring to a program we had put in place with the North Carolina Jaycees - the Prisoner Rehabilitation Program. It was a good program and I was proud of what we had accomplished with it, but I was not interested in being in any management or administrative position with the program.

I said, "Governor, I've made arrangements for housing here in Raleigh, but I don't have to use them and I'm just not interested in being involved in the prisoner rehabilitation program."

During my response I had stood up, and the Governor, who was always frank and plain spoken, said, "Sit down, Bill. You don't know what I have in mind."

Governor Hodges went on to detail a program that could not have been more tailor-made for my experience and expertise in business. The prisoners in the North Carolina prison system had primarily been engaged in highway maintenance. However, the United States Congress had passed a law restricting their being used for that purpose. With 8,000 prisoners in the system, the state was looking at a large problem if it couldn't find something for these inmates to do that would keep them busy and out of trouble. There were a few prisoners already involved in an industrial program manufacturing automobile license plates and in several other industries.

"I want the prison industries program to be expanded and be put on a sound, business-like basis, and that's what I want you to do. This program has a lot of possibilities. We can teach the inmates skills which they do not now possess. That'll equip them to be effectively and productively employed when they are released. Further, we can manufacture products which the state is now purchasing and save a lot of tax dollars."

As Paul Johnson had said at the Christmas party, Governor Hodges' administration was doing work I would find interesting and important. This plan made a lot of sense and interested me; actually it challenged me and these were the types of problems I liked to work on. My official title was the Assistant Director of the North Carolina Prison Department, in charge of the Prison Industries Program.

I was blessed with a group of enthusiastic and bright individuals who were already in place ready to work on this project, a fact which contributed greatly to the success of the programs we were putting in place. Every week we would meet around a conference table and generate ideas and provide feedback on what we had already put in place.

While I worked as assistant director, we expanded the prisons' metal working capabilities to include manufacturing stainless steel equipment for kitchens for the various state-operated facilities. We expanded and improved the print plant and clothing manufacturing. We manufactured mattresses as well as uniforms, and many other items in our sewing plants. In our chemical plant, we manufactured soaps, detergents, and a variety of other cleaning materials. The paint plant manufactured outstanding products, including all types of paints, stains, and varnishes. We named the products manufactured Tarstan, an acronym for Tarheel State Industries. We also developed a logo which would make the items appear more like standard brands, manufactured by traditional companies to avoid the stigma of prison-made products.

By coordinating with the Division of Purchase and Contract, we were able to promote the products and sell directly to the state agencies. The Great Depression created the system that allowed us to accomplish this. In 1931, most of the counties in North Carolina went bankrupt, and they had outstanding bonds which they could not honor. The North Carolina General Assembly passed sweeping legislation to provide more stability and efficiency for governing bodies throughout the state. One piece of legislation created a centralized purchasing department, which reported directly to the governor. This purchasing act required all government facilities, state and local, public schools, hospitals and any other organization of government to direct their purchases through the North Carolina Division of Purchase and Contract.

After a year of re-organization, expansion, and promotion in the Prison Department, we were able to bid on State contracts through the Division of Purchase and Contract, and we increased our sales to state agencies substantially. We were saving the state agencies over a million dollars a year over what they had been paying for these products. Further, we were able to teach skills to inmates being released, which enabled them to be gainfully employed once they were released, a key to reducing the recidivism rate. We had a waiting list for inmates being released from our print plant and metal working operation.

Over the years, the Division of Purchase and Contract had become somewhat politicized and inefficient. Governor Hodges decided that reorganizing this division and putting it on a sound business-like basis was next on my job list. I'm not sure that he knew until after he had appointed me Director of the Division that I had purchasing agent experience. Nevertheless, it did improve my ability to function and achieve the results he desired.

This division had some excellent, dedicated employees as well who were very receptive to developing and implementing plans to increase the effectiveness of their service.

Previously, in characteristic bureaucratic fashion, the division had been under the supervision of the budget department. Also, there was a board appointed by the Legislature and the Governor to pass on requested and recommended purchases. With its high degree of centralized purchasing, North Carolina generated a huge volume of purchases, second in volume only to the federal government.

I felt, not for the first time, that God had put me in the right place at the right time. Doing God's work wasn't always about direct ministry, but was always about doing one's best with what God had provided. I certainly felt this was the case with the work I did while serving in this administration.

While working as the director, and with the input of the staff, many new policies were established that greatly improved the efficiency of the Purchase and Contract division. For example, the budget department required that state vehicles remain in service on an average of four to five years, or better, adjusted somewhat by the mileage. The use of vehicles over that long period of time meant that large amounts were spent on tires, batteries, parts, and repairs. During World War II, the federal government had established what amounted to an excise tax on automobiles. However, purchases by government agencies were exempt from this tax. Because of this exemption and the large volume of vehicles which the state purchased, the state could buy at or below dealer's cost. After a detailed study considering these factors, we determined that we could trade in state vehicles after one year of service and actually sell them for what we had paid for them. However, upon discussing this with the Governor and the Board and other advisors, we determined that this would not be in the best interest of the state because it would be unfair to the car dealers. We established a policy of permitting a vehicle to be replaced after 15 to 18 months, depending on mileage and maintenance records. This literally began saving the state millions of dollars in maintenance and equipment which required replacement. I might also add this contributed considerably to state employees' morale.

Some of the improvements were easier to implement because, with the Governor's recommendation, the legislature had created the Department of Administration which took the Division of Purchase and Contract out from the Budget Department and put it under an administration that was specifically concerned with state services. This was one of many programs which we developed and implemented, and again I emphasize the credit is due to the outstanding staff which I inherited.

The division received a lot of publicity, and Governor Hodges had requests from a number of states asking for confirmation on North Carolina's purchasing program. He volunteered my services and I spent sometime visiting, studying and recommending improvements to the purchasing policies of Florida, Ohio, South Carolina, and several other states. I served as the Vice-President of the States Purchasing Agents Association.

During those years, it seemed as if one job led to another. After a couple of years or so, the Director of the Commerce Division of the Department of Conservation and Development resigned, and Governor Hodges appointed me Director of the Division. I had been very interested in industrial development. As President of the North Carolina Jaycees, I was asked to speak at a Chamber of Commerce banquet in Franklin, North Carolina. The morning following the banquet, the President of the Chamber of Commerce took me on a tour, and one of the offices we visited was the local newspaper. The editor of the paper, during our visit with him, made a startling statement. He said, "You know, there are actually more people age 21 to 35 who were born in Macon County now living in Detroit than living here in the county."

We discussed how North Carolina was experiencing a severe brain drain. There were no job opportunities available for young men and women in the county, so upon graduation from high school, they would follow their sisters, brothers, and cousins to

Michigan to find employment. Those who were privileged enough to go to college had virtually no potential for employment in the county. Economic growth in the county, and the state in general, was severely impeded.

We decided to capitalize on the fact that the state of North Carolina was experiencing the transition of moving from an agrarian economy to a manufacturing and industrialized economy. North Carolina had the highest number of farms of any state in the United States, and, although we were about tenth in size, this large number of farms meant that our farms were relatively small. This phenomenon developed because out agricultural industry had as its basis the cultivation of tobacco. Tobacco at that time produced a high dollar per acre yield, which meant that a farmer could exist on a relatively small farm compared to those states whose agricultural industry was supported by grain crops, such as wheat and corn. As the cultivation of tobacco became increasingly mechanized, less and less labor was required to cultivate and harvest the crops. This was producing surplus labor for which there was no employment in North Carolina. This led to the migration of our work force to other states.

This became both a curse and a blessing: it was draining a lot of our bright, young citizens, citizens the state had spent large sums in educating and preparing for adulthood. At the same time, this produced a blessing in the availability of a large pool of intelligent, trainable, potential employees. Governor Umstead had addressed this situation very forcefully during his campaign for Governor, and Mr. Hodges, when he became governor, was equally or even more so dedicated. It became one of the major objectives of his administration.

I had been involved to some minor degree with the Governor in some of the plans for the state's economic development program. Governor Hodges was interested not only in attracting business from out of state, but he wanted to encourage the development and expansion of industries within the state. There was no major venture capital organization available, and many small businesses could not expand or be developed because of a lack of capital. He developed and the legislature passed enabling legislation to form an organization known as the Business Development Corporation of North Carolina.

The purpose of this organization was to provide consulting and financial guidance to existing industries, and to provide loans for the development of new industries. To provide the capital required this organization became a lending institution. A million dollars worth of stock was subscribed, and I was involved in securing commitments for a good part of this. Because this was an idea believed in and because I had spent years cultivating business connections, I had little problem successfully securing funds. My efforts were directed mainly through the

North Carolina Junior Chamber of Commerce chapters. I was appointed to the board which was created to supervise the activities of the corporation. Therefore, I had some up-to-date appreciation for the economic development of the state. The previous Director of the Commerce Division had done an outstanding job with the encouragement and expectations which Governor Hodges constantly promoted. I again inherited a very qualified staff of intelligent, experienced public servants.

We were able to bring to the program some new ideas and be a part of planning for the establishment of programs and agencies that were undergirded by and complimented the state's industrial development efforts. For example, while we found many companies willing to consider moving to North Carolina, one of the objections was the lack of skilled, trained employees. To help alleviate this objection, legislation was recommended by the Governor and passed to create the ability of the counties and state to begin Industrial Training Centers. These centers were initially begun to train employees for Industry and Commerce. There were certain academic programs required to be an integral part of the centers. These Industrial Training Centers have over the years developed into the Community College program that has been such a tremendous asset to our state.

I also had a very modest part in the efforts to bring the Research Triangle Park into reality, the success of which speaks eloquently of Governor Hodges' vision and mission for the state. Mr. Hodges was a very intelligent, attractive communicator who was totally committed to the Industrial Development Program of the state. I was fortunate in having the relationship I had with Mr. Hodges. I could go to him direct and he was always available and cooperative. Although he was a man of dignity, he agreed to take a shower in a Dacron suit to promote a Dupont plant in North Carolina. The picture was reproduced on the cover of "Time Magazine," a fact which gave our promotion efforts a big boost.

While we were focused on bringing new industry to North Carolina, we did not overlook promoting existing industry. One of our programs to promote existing industries created a showplace of products manufactured in North Carolina. What began as an idea from one of the staff members developed into organizing and producing the first state trade fair in the United States. I knew nothing about a trade fair, so I sent some of our staff to Europe to attend and study the various trade fairs on the continent. I went to New York and arranged a conference with the President of the International Trade Fair Association, a distinguished gentleman by the name of Walter Snitow. He was very generous with his time and spent many hours with me during my several visits to his office. He came to North Carolina and helped us organize and instructed us on how to conduct a trade fair.

We have a wide variety of manufacturers in North Carolina who made an amazing number of products.

We solicited these companies to display their products during the trade fair. We invited purchasing agents from throughout the United States and some foreign markets to attend and be informed regarding the products of these manufacturing companies. We were successful in selling all of the display space. The trade fair was held at a new exhibition building next to the Charlotte Coliseum. We gave cities which had exhibition space available the opportunity to present a proposal to us to host the trade fair. Charlotte's proposal was selected, and we received excellent cooperation from the Charlotte community. We held the trade fair during a two-week period, and approximately 200,000 attended. Although our efforts were directed towards creating additional business for North Carolina manufacturers, with prudent administration, we actually made a profit. Not only did it not cost the state any money, but we turned over $125,000 to the state at the end of the fair.

After Governor Hodges finished his term, he was succeeded by Terry Sanford, who asked me to stay on with his administration. I agreed but only stayed on for a year or so. I was pleased over what I had managed to accomplish during my work with Governor Hodges. Two of the three years I was Director of the Division of Commerce and Industry, we won the award from the National Association of Industrial

Realtors, an organization I was very active in, for having the most outstanding industrial development program in the United States. The Division of Commerce and Industry later was made a full department, and is now recognized as the Department of Commerce.

When Governor Hodges left office, President Kennedy appointed him Secretary of the U.S. Department of Commerce. During a visit, Secretary Hodges offered me the opportunity of becoming an assistant Secretary of the Department of Commerce. I was flattered but respectfully declined. I had been involved in politics for several years and was feeling the pull to return to the business community. I also knew that a political life would not suit Dot. While I enjoyed and took pride from the work I had been a part of, it wasn't worth any negative impact to my family to continue in Washington D.C.

I had faced this issue once before, choosing a political life or making the unselfish choice to put Dot's desires above my own desires and ambitions. I had planned while involved in the Jaycees to become President of the U.S. Jaycees. In fact, I had been approached by a delegation that claimed they had enough votes committed to elect me President if I would agree to run. Winning the post would have meant moving to the Jaycees Headquarters in Tulsa, Oklahoma, a move I knew Dot would not be in favor of. I also knew Dot had no desire to be the wife of a politician. My initial plan was to run for

Congress after my term of President of the Jaycees was over by using the contacts I had made in that position to advance my political career. I fancied myself a different type of politician, a sort of "Mr. Smith Goes to Washington" type.

I never told Dot about these plans or the possibility of becoming the Jaycees President. Although I had very much desired to proceed with the plan, I decided to decline and trust God for our future, a future which would be more satisfying to Dot. Until this day, I have never told her of the proposal or my reason for rejecting it. I did not want her to feel she had stood in the way of my future.

Chapter 18

Personal Politics

I N THE SHORT TIME I CONTINUED ON WITH Governor Sanford, I became aware of a legalistic trend to my faith, and Governor Sanford's reaction to it should have been an early warning sign. About ten years earlier, the mother of a young man I had known told me that her son, who was an alcoholic, had given up drinking alcohol because he wanted to be able to have fun and be prosperous like me, and obviously I had done it without drinking. That I had inspired this young man to turn away from drinking made me appreciate the fact that I had quit even social drinking. Drinking in the military was as much a part of life as wearing a uniform and smoking cigarettes. This was also during a time when cocktail hour was a national pastime in nearly every home. From that time on, I refused to drink because of my faith, finding Biblical evidence to support my decision. Dot and I had fairly legalistic attitudes to begin with, which can unfortunately lead a Christian to overlook the larger aspect of God's grace and God's desire that we enjoy life in favor of paying attention to keeping in line with every rule.

At a dinner function with Governor Sanford, the Governor was taking orders for cocktails. Governor Sanford remarked when he came to me, "Oh no, none for Bill. He doesn't drink any alcohol, you know." I felt embarrassed.

The next day I walked into the Governor's office and said, "Now Terry, you know why I don't drink, don't you?" This was a rhetorical question because, frankly, everyone knew why I didn't drink. Hidden in my explanations of why I didn't drink were not so subtle suggestions on how to live a better Christian life. I didn't see back then how self-righteous I was being.

Terry replied, "Yes, Bill. I know why you don't drink."

"Okay, then," I told him, and turned and left. Legalism had a way of making one feel that actions like Governor Sanford's showed I was doing the right thing – obviously he felt compelled to embarrass me to hide the fact that he knew he was wrong in drinking himself, I reasoned. In reality, I was not unlike the Pharisees that Jesus complained about. It was the spirit in which one drank, or the priority drinking had in one's life that mattered, not the fact that a person had a glass of wine with dinner. It took a long time before I finally saw this and began to relax a bit.

Chapter 19

A Return to Business

AFTER LEAVING GOVERNMENT WORK, I managed to seamlessly move back into the private business sector in advertising. As the Director of the Commerce Division, I had been asked to comment on the state advertising since a good portion of it related to industrial development. In that capacity, I became acquainted with the Account Executive of Bennett Advertising, who was in charge of the state account. He advised me that Mr. Bennett, who founded Bennett Advertising in 1922, was going to retire and was interested in selling Bennett Advertising. Bennett Advertising was one of the oldest and most respected advertising agencies in the Southeast. He had a staff of very competent, experienced advertising professionals and an impressive stable of accounts.

I contacted Mr. Bennett and after a month or so of negotiations, I bought the agency.

I had had an interest in advertising ever since my college days, when I spent some time with a large international advertising agency in New York. I became active in the American Association of Advertising Agencies, where I became an officer, and our agency was recognized for some outstanding work for our clients. My family and I moved to High Point, North Carolina, the headquarters of Bennett Advertising, and we became active in the community. We served in various social and civic organizations. It was quite natural that I became interested in the affairs of High Point College where I had graduated. I served as President of the Alumni Association and was the director of the first multi-million dollar campaign for the college endowment fund. I was elected to the College Board of Trustees and am still a member of that board.

By the time we moved to High Point, our two children, Faithe and Chip, were born. The house we purchased when we moved to High Point was modest but adequate. However, after several years, we built our dream home which gave me the opportunity to pursue an interest that I had not had the time or proper facilities to enjoy. I've always loved flowers, so I became a very serious gardener in landscaping our large lot. The hobby provided me with much needed relaxation and time with the children out-side.

The ad agency was meeting our expectations, but nothing of any great significance. We had offices in Raleigh and Charlotte which I visited on a regular basis. One day when I visited the Charlotte office, the receptionist gave me a message that someone had been trying to reach me and had a left a number for me to call. I called the number and a man answered and when I identified myself, he said, "Bill, my name is Delbert Bolding and I went to school with you in Asheboro. I don't expect you to remember me but the press has kept me informed of your activities. I live in Myrtle Beach, SC and I'm here with a friend, and we need the service of an advertising and public relations agency."

We made an appointment for lunch, and at that time, they informed me they had an option to purchase Bald Head Island. Mr. Frank Sherrill, the owner of the S&W cafeteria chain, who had owned the island since 1939, had become convinced that at his age he was not going to be able to develop it as he had envisioned. In fact, he had contracted to sell it to Charlie Fraser, the developer of Hilton Head Island. Mr. Fraser had run into a lot of criticism and opposition from the environmentalists and had dropped his offer to purchase. So Mr. Sherrill was looking for a buyer. They said they needed someone to handle their public relations and enable them to move forward with their plans to develop the island.

They offered me an attractive proposal, in effect, offered to give me one-third interest in the project if I would join them.

I knew something about the project since a lot had been in the press regarding Mr. Fraser's plans. I realized that they had a problem that would require making some environmental commitments regarding the development. If those commitments were not honored, it would adversely reflect on those associated with the development. I was concerned that I did not know anything about these men who had an additional partner in Southport, NC – a gentleman by the name of Jimmy Prevette. I told them that I would have to think about their proposal and get back to them.

I investigated the background of Boling, Todd, and Prevette, something I did with anyone I was considering engaging in business with. I had no problem walking away from business deals if there was anything shady or underhanded in a partner's past. I also had a very strong sense of stewardship to the environment because of my faith specifically. I believed that God had provided the earth to us in trust, to use it not to abuse it. To the best of my ability, I was able to determine that the three men were good businessmen who had some financial resources and were known to be fair in their dealings. I had learned that Mr. Prevette in particular was a very respected attorney in the Southport area. He was on the board of the North Carolina Baptist Association and a Regent of Wake Forest University.

With this information, I met with them and agreed to become a partner, provided I had complete authority to manage and represent the company. I had some experience with the development business since our agency had worked for several developers, handling their planning and promotion. They agreed and we entered into an agreement. The option to purchase required paying Mr. Sherill $5.6 million for the some 11,000 acres. These 11,000 acres included some questionable marsh lands. Actually, there was something just over 3,000 acres of high ground that could be developed in a profitable and responsible fashion.

I knew more about Bald Head Island than I initially divulged to my partners. I continually found it interesting how God directed my life with different experiences that later would prove valuable. When I was director of the Commerce Division, I received a call from Governor Hodges one day to come and meet with him. At that meeting, he told me he wanted me to go and visit Smith Island, which at that time was its official name, but commonly called Bald Head Island. He said Mr. Frank Sherrill owned the island and had a plan for developing it and wanted the state to build a road to the island. He said, "I have no idea whether it's justified; I want you to go and give me a recommendation." I thought of Colonel Liversedge with his frequent comment, "Henderson, you need this experience."

Mr. Sherrill had originally tried to sell the property as a location for the United Nations. In fact, it was my understanding that it was the second place choice, runner up to the New York location. Following that, Mr. Sherrill had spent a lot of time and money planning a complete community on Bald Head Island, utilizing part of the property for high-tech type industry, as well as residential and resort facilities. I made an appointment to meet Mr. Sherrill at Southport, and we spent a day visiting the island. Our guide was the caretaker on Bald Head Island, and he was the son of the last Coast Guard Captain stationed on Bald Head Island. Therefore, we experienced not only the physical attributes of the island, but also a lot of its rich history, including when Edward Teach (Blackbeard) used it as a staging area for his forays and attacks on merchant ships.

I had never been on Bald Head Island and was amazed at its beauty, including 14 miles of unspoiled beach and the maritime forest. I was particularly surprised and impressed on finding tropical vegetation, including palm trees and other lush tropical plants, which, to the best of my knowledge, did not grow north of Charleston, SC. It's surmised that since Bald Head Island juts out from the mainland and is the closest point to the gulfstream, the warm waters of the gulfstream have some moderating effect on the weather. It's true it is warmer during the winter on Bald Head Island than it is back on the mainland.

After my visit to Bald Head, I had discussed the feasibility of a highway with the engineers of the highway department and the estimated cost, and evaluated Mr. Sherrill's plans with our staff. We concluded that such a development would be beneficial to the state, but it was not economically or politically feasible (due to the environmental concerns), which I reported to Governor Hodges.

With my three partners, we engaged an engineering firm, the Freeman Brothers, to survey and, under our direction, craft a development plan for the island, including a construction schedule and financial pro forma. We made plans to incorporate the environmental considerations into our plans. I formed an Ecological Advisory Committee to help guide us in our planning. This nine-member committee was the first committee of its kind, to my knowledge, which solicited the input of scientists representing various disciplines. Most of the members of the committee were professors or adjunct professors at North Carolina State University, the University of NC at Chapel Hill, and Duke University.

Upon the completion of the master plan and financial pro forma, we developed a sales program which was intended to raise a substantial portion of the money to purchase the island. Our staff at Bennett Advertising created an attractive, comprehensive slide presentation which told the history and romance of Bald Head Island, as well as the plans for responsible development of this jewel of nature. We put together a package to be offered to potential buyers, consisting of a proposed beach lot and a dune or forest lot. The price of the package was $25,000. We contacted friends in some 12 or 15 North Carolina communities and asked them to invite four or five couples, who they thought might have an interest, to their home for refreshments and a presentation of the slide show. My staff and I were present at these affairs which met with surprising success. We wrote contracts for the purchase of some $3.2 million dollars of lots. After construction began, we invited these potential buyers to attend an on-site visit, and after touring the island, they selected their properties.

In those initial phases, we actually closed $3.1 million of the $3.2 million worth of contracts. This was particularly impressive, in that only a minimal amount of construction had been accomplished and we had experienced serious opposition to our plans. In fact, it took us months and several trips to Washington to secure approval to build a dock at Bald Head Island.

I believe God was watching out for my family because during the early stages, I maintained my residence in High Point, traveling back and forth to Bald Head Island. I realized that at some point in the near future, the project would require daily attention. In short, I would have to relocate. I prayed repeatedly that God would help me secure a home in the vicinity. That summer, we rented a house at the northern end of Long Beach, where the family enjoyed the summer at the beach. I think we entertained every friend and acquaintance we had ever known during that summer.

Approaching the end of the summer, a gentleman by the name of Hugh Morton, whom I had known for several years and who was an outstanding photographer, came down to Bald Head to take some pictures. I accompanied him on his tour of the island, at which time he reminded me that he was developing Grandfather Mountain. He, like I, had been commuting back and forth. He had reached the decision to move to the Grandfather Mountain area and planned to sell his home in Wilmington, North Carolina. He asked if we would be interested in buying it. I made an appointment for Dot and me to visit their home, and we both liked it. It was very livable, and I was particularly attracted to the beautiful landscaping and garden. He told me the purchase price, which was reasonable, and we agreed to the purchase.

We had one small hurdle to jump before the purchase was final, but I believed if this was where God wanted us, it would work out. Hugh had promised a doctor friend the first right of refusal if they ever decided to sell. A few days later, Hugh called us to say that his doctor friend had decided to build rather than buy their home. We put our house in High Point on the market, and it sold immediately. We moved into our new home on Live Oak Parkway in Wilmington, with little problems other than the fact that our children weren't too happy about moving.

Not long after we moved, I received a call from a friend in Greensboro that led to the second incident with a plane ride that could have ended my life. My friend and I had served together on the board of Piedmont Aero, a fixed base operation based at the Greensboro HighPoint Winston Salem Airport. He asked if I would be willing to visit an old hunting lodge he and a group of friends had bought on the coast. The state wanted to include it in a preservation program and had appraised it at what he thought was low. He wanted me to evaluate the value of the property if they utilized it for a resort development. He said he would send a plane from Piedmont Aero to take me to the lodge and then take me wherever I wanted to go.

The plane picked me up early in the morning at the Brunswick county airport, and we flew to the lodge. There was a dirt landing strip where we landed. After spending the day walking and studying the land, we got on the plane and took off. Unfortunately the pilot misjudged or a gust of wind moved us because we went from the hard dirt of the runway to the soft sand as we began to get airborne. The plane veered off the runway and crashed into the underbrush. It was a brand new KingAir and the pilot was a veteran air force pilot; however, neither of these facts saved us from a freak accident. No one was seriously hurt. We took a boat over to the mainland, and leased a plane at the New Bern airport, flying on to Greensboro High Point airport, where I had told my wife to pick me up that afternoon. I arrived after midnight to a nervous Dot who had been waiting for several hours.

Every day working on the Bald Head Island was a constant battle. It was during this time that I struggled a bit with God, wondering why the deal was not working out well, as if good behavior on my part guaranteed a positive outcome in every endeavor. Not only did we have to contend with the problems of development, but the environmentalists. Those who didn't want to see the property developed at all were constantly complaining to the regulatory agencies, encouraging them to disapprove every request we submitted. Governor Bob Scott was constantly besieged by reporters in an effort to determine the state's attitude regarding development.

I went to see the Governor, whom I had known for some time and explained to him our plans. With the approval of my partners, I offered the state the opportunity to buy the property from us for exactly what we had paid for it, plus our out-of-pocket expenses that were modest. He quickly stated that the state did not have any money to buy the property, and I gathered from our conversation that he was not interested in promoting the availability of funds through the General Assembly. Frankly, I think Governor Scott, whose family owned a fair bit of property in Alamance County, appreciated the right of a property owner to utilize his property, provided the utilization was responsible and did not adversely affect his neighbors or the environment. However, this was a time when environmentalists were very vocal and politically he was not about to, nor could he, support the private development of Bald Head Island.

I think the anti-developers and environmentalists realized it was not economically feasible for the state to buy the property, so their intentions were to discourage developers, such as they had done with Mr. Frazer and Mr. Sherrill, who would eventually have to give or sell the property to the state at a distressed price. I endured the negative editorials and political cartoons. In fact, I considered them rather humorous. Frankly, they only increased my resolve to develop Bald Head Island in a responsible manner that was still profitable to our investors and unique for its owners.

The only alternative I could see for the island property was to leave it undeveloped, suffering the ravages of time and weather, and to a considerable extent, destroying much of its natural attributes. I ascertained from Mr. Sherrill that he had no intentions of considering donating the island to the state, and he could well afford not to sell the property at some severely discounted price.

While I was prevailing under all these circumstances, our financial plans were being jeopardized by continued delays and legal fees. My partners and I had funded the project to the extent that we could borrow sufficient funds to purchase and initiate our development. However, we had to incur some debt because of the various problems we were encountering. Further, we had to adjust our plans to reality, which meant we would not begin receiving a return on our investment as quickly as we had anticipated. This caused some consternation among our partners and board members. We had organized a company called Carolina Cape Fear Corporation and elected a board of well qualified businessmen. The board and some of the investors were beginning to have a difference of opinion regarding our development plans. I had no desire to remain a part of anything which might become controversial, or where the commitments I made regarding the development might be modified or disregarded. Therefore, when a business man made me an offer to purchase my interest, I gave it serious consideration and eventually agreed to sell my interest.

Chapter 20

Unique Opportunities

A<small>S</small> I <small>SHUT THE DOOR ON ONE OPPOR</small>tu nity, God was opening the door on another. I received a call from Governor Jim Holshauser, a Republican, who had succeeded Governor Scott.

"Bill, I know you're in Raleigh frequently. I'd like to get together to discuss an idea I have."

He didn't say what the idea was, which had me a bit curious, especially since I was a registered Democrat at the time, though I did support conservative causes.

"I'm on my way out the door to go to a conference, and then I promised Dot a few days vacation. She's actually out in the car waiting to leave."

"Will you pass through Charlotte on your way? If you can, I'll have an associate, Joe Millsaps, meet with you there."

Governor Holshauser's representative met with me at a restaurant in Charlotte because the Governor wanted to appoint me to the North Carolina Zoological Board. The board had been created to locate and establish a state zoo. Red Pope, Jr., a member of the Raleigh Junior Chamber of Commerce, promoted the Raleigh Jaycees sponsoring the development of the zoo. The Jaycees sponsored a pro-football game, with the proceeds dedicated to begin the development of the zoo. Mr. Pope and the Raleigh Jaycees began to realize that the potential for the project had such state-wide implications that it would challenge the energy and the resources of their local chapter. The idea was then presented to the North Carolina General Assembly, who created a Zoological Board. This board traveled to zoos throughout the United States, gathering information on what type and how to develop and maintain a quality facility. Various locations in the state were considered and a site in Asheboro, NC, in Randolph County was selected. A Zoological Society was provided for in legislation and charged with the responsibility for providing financial support for the state's effort to develop the zoo.

The idea of the zoo appealed to me, as one of their main objectives was to be responsible for the animals, not simply to showcase them. The decision had been made that the zoo would be a natural-habitat zoo – that is, as much as possible, to put the animals in their normal environment and not keep them caged up. This meant a large area would be needed, not only to accommodate the natural habitat concept but also to have separate areas for separate continents.

They committed to purchase approximately 1100 acres just outside of Asheboro, which was where I came in. A portion of the property had been contributed through the efforts of local citizens. The legislature budgeted some money; however, the Zoological Society was short approximately $750,000. Construction had begun on the zoo, and unfortunately for the state, it was being planned on property which had not been purchased and paid for. Governor Holshauser did not know this. He knew there was a need to raise a significant amount to augment what he felt the North Carolina General Assembly would provide - that was the challenge he wanted me to respond to.

Always eager for a challenge and a problem to solve, I agreed to be elected to the Board of the Zoological Society. Being a member of the Board seemed more appropriate and allowed me to be more effective, free of any political implications since the society's board members were elected by the society's members and not appointed by the General Assembly or the Governor.

We faced a daunting task because something over $600,000 had to be paid in a relatively short time to secure the land on which the first phase of development was occurring. Billy Carmichael of Chapel Hill, who was a member of the Board of the Zoological Society, suggested we have a 24-hour telethon to cover all of North Carolina and raise the necessary funds. Billy, who owned an advertising and public relations company, organized the telethon and was able to secure the cooperation of the various television stations to have complete coverage of the state. He secured the availability of a number of outstanding celebrities, as well as zoo enthusiasts and zoo supporters and produced an entertaining and successful telethon. While, the society's main efforts were originally to provide funds for animals because the state was limited in what the general assembly would provide through the state budget, the society also solicited funds for physical facilities and other needs. These efforts were coordinated with the North Carolina Zoological Board. Through friends I knew at R. J. Reynolds Tobacco Company, we presented the idea of Reynolds contributing money for a world-class aviary. Reynolds pledged somewhere between 1.2-1.5 million dollars for the construction and equipping of the aviary, which became the first significant facility at the zoo.

I served on the board for some 12 years and was Chairman of the Board the last eight years. I realized I had made all the contributions I could, and so I did not stand for re-election. I was surprised and embarrassed when the board passed a resolution naming the Zoological Board headquarters building in my honor. I certainly didn't desire it, nor did I deserve it. I remembered an occasion when I was in Governor Hodges office and a delegation from the University of North Carolina at Chapel Hill, with a great deal of enthusiasm and excitement, advised him that they were planning to name a large new facility at the University honoring him. He quickly responded that he didn't want any part of it, saying that buildings were named for dead men and heroes, and he wasn't either one. I guess I felt somewhat like he did.

No temptation has seized you except what is common to man. And God is faithful; he will not let you be tempted beyond what you can bear. But when you are tempted, he will also provide a way out so that you can stand up under it.   *1 Cor 10:13*

Chapter 21

The Hardships of Real Estate

THE BALD HEAD ISLAND ISSUE RESURfaced during this time. While I had sold my interest, I had agreed to finance a large portion of it, and the purchaser defaulted on his obligation. Unfortunately, the company by then had deteriorated financially and the property was taken over by one of the lenders. The on-going problems with Bald Head and the consulting business I was also doing for lending institutions who had loaned money for real estate development served as a backdrop while I started my own real estate development company, which would lead to one of the greatest mishaps of my business life.

My office was in Wilmington, North Carolina, but on one of my frequent trips to Raleigh, I stopped in to see a friend, Jim Harrington, who was the

Secretary of the North Carolina Department of Commerce. He said he didn't think Governor Holshauser would be running for another term, and since his appointment would be expiring, he was looking for career opportunities outside of state government. Jim had been President of a company which owned and operated the outstanding Pinehurst resort; therefore, he was very familiar with the development business. Jim was a very bright fellow who had a lot of the talents that I lacked. I told him that I was in the consulting business and had more business than I could look after, and would he be interested in joining me as a partner. We entered into discussions regarding this possibility.

I was in Raleigh frequently because one of my clients had a development in Cary, and they had engaged me to handle their promotion and marketing. They had a beautiful piece of property consisting of over 1,000 acres in a very desirable location. Tom Adams, one of the owners, was an attorney who specialized in real estate; however, he had never done any development, and had planned, along with his brothers who were partners, the first Planned Unit Development in North Carolina called Kildaire Farms. The Planned Unit Development idea accommodated not only housing, but recreation, shopping and other community services. It was an excellent plan; however, instead of phasing it, Tom constructed much of the infrastructure for the whole project. Naturally, the debt for the acquisition and development was substantial because of not phasing the infrastructure. The interest on the debt required a sales volume higher than what the market could sustain. Since we were just coming out of the high interest period when interest on houses reached 16%, many potential homeowners were denied the ability to purchase. Kildaire Farms needed some extraordinary promotion and marketing to enable the owners to survive.

We began an aggressive advertising and promotion campaign and recruited a stable of quality custom builders. We had breakfast with these builders once a month to review our plans and solicit their opinions and participation. We had weekly tours of the project, bringing in the brokers and sales people of area real estate marketing and sales companies.

Once again, God's providence helped with our relocation to Raleigh. Out of the blue, I had a call from a gentleman that I had a casual acquaintance with. He said he was on the North Carolina Utility Commission; his term was going to be up shortly, he explained, and he intended to return to his law practice in Wilmington. He knew we had bought the Morton house in Wilmington and said they had a nice livable house in Raleigh, and would there be some interest in our exchanging houses. It sounded like a unique idea. My wife, Dot, thought the Raleigh house was acceptable, so we had appraisals made for each home and worked out a satisfactory exchange. We saved any real estate commission and the inconvenience of showing our homes. Our family moved to Raleigh and we settled in our new home.

The economy was improving, which was reflected in our sales at Kildaire Farms. Tom Adams, the managing partner of Kildaire Farms, invited Dot and me to have dinner with him and his wife. At dinner, Tom introduced us to a man by the name of Sy Vogel. Sy was associated with the Harlon Company from Texas, and he said that they were interested in moving their real estate development office to Raleigh. He said he was looking for someone to help him locate land to purchase. In the course of several meetings, he expressed an interest in Kildaire Farms, which had been bought by two gentlemen, Walter Davis and Jim Harrington, whom I had introduced to Tom Adams.

Jim Harrington and I had been considering becoming associated, and during our negotiations I had suggested to him the possibility of Kildaire Farms being for sale. He expressed an interest and I negotiated a sale of Kildaire Farms to Walter Davis and Jim Harrington. Initially, I was going to participate in ownership; however, Walter Davis preferred that I maintain an independent position, and we agreed upon a satisfactory contract for me to handle the sales and marketing of Kildaire Farms.

I approached Jim Harrington with the idea of their selling Kildaire Farms to the Harlon Company. We negotiated a contract which was attractive to both the buyer and seller. I received what became a very valuable property in Kildaire as compensation for negotiating the contract and satisfaction for losing my contract to promote and market the project. I was able to subsequently sell portions of the property that I had received. The income from these sales added to what I had been able to accumulate from other ventures gave me an investment fund which enabled me to start my own real estate brokerage and development company, something I had been working towards for some time.

The Raleigh market was beginning to be very active, and we were able to secure the help of some of the triangle's more successful real estate professionals. Combined with their experience and my resources, we purchased a number of properties. In most cases, we would purchase a property and get the property planned and zoned and then sell it. Our holding period was relatively short. Therefore, we turned our money over quickly. As business continued to grow, we formed a company, W.R. Henderson and Associates. There were six partners involved in the company, and we had some eight to ten brokers and salesmen. While this company was successful, some of the partners decided they wanted to venture off on their own. They either resigned or I bought them out; soon I was the sole owner.

During this period of time, I did a lot of business with Sy Vogel. Through him and with him, we bought and sold over $50 million worth of land.

I was approached by a group from Florida who had been in the development business in Indiana and Florida and owned apartment projects in several other states. They approached me with the idea of their becoming a part of W. R. Henderson and Associates. One of the main considerations for me was the fact that they proposed to have excellent relationships with a number of financial institutions. While I had a very satisfactory relationship with local financial institutions, there was a limit as to how much lending they could do to one developer.

The Florida group was very ambitious and we devised a long-range plan for our company and new partners. We visited with them in Florida and investigated them to the best of our ability. They did appear to have the financial contacts; however, their development experience was limited. Dot had the occasion to meet them as well; her opinion was less than favorable, though she couldn't put an exact reason to her feelings.

"Bill," she told me, "there's something wrong with them. They appear fine on the surface, but I have a concern. Something doesn't feel right."

Dot didn't often offer her opinion. She listened a great deal when I used her as a sounding board – I talked out loud, and she stood by listening so I didn't feel like a fool talking to myself. In truth, I valued her opinion when she gave it, but in this case, I valued the financial contacts more. I agreed with her assessment, but I couldn't put my finger on the problem.

"I think it will work out if I keep an eye on all the deals. They're good Christians. All their past deals have been solid. I don't think there'll be any problems," I assured her, confident in my ability to control the outcome in this case.

We proceeded with a business arrangement and developed a number of properties in the Research Triangle Park area and on the east and west coasts of Florida; we also purchased and rehabilitated a large apartment complex in Houston, Texas. All was good, for a time.

Most of their financial contacts and mine were with savings and loan companies. Savings and Loan companies had initially been created to assist people in buying homes with the S&L providing the financing. Since historically they had been involved in this type of lending, they tended to be more favorably inclined to finance real estate development projects. Some banks became involved, but their regulations were not as flexible as the S&L companies. Because of these reasons, we did most of our financing with Savings and Loan companies.

The almost insatiable appetite of my partners caused our company to acquire a large number of projects, and we were able to do so because the savings and loans were very aggressive with their lending policies. We enjoyed a good reputation with them. We leveraged as much as we could in financing the project; therefore, we had a lot of debt.

However, that worked for us because the market was good and we were able to meet our obligations.

We traditionally borrowed 80 to 90 percent to acquire and develop a project. We were never guilty of the practice used by some developers who would get an aggressive appraisal of the property that exceeded the purchase price and borrow 120%, plus or minus, of the purchase price. They would pocket the excess money above the purchase price, and while this nefarious practice was feasible during an accelerating market, when some tax law changes were made and a blip in the economy resulted in a slowdown of the growth of sales in real estate, the developers were not able to honor their commitments on their loans. They had no resources or equity to cover a period when income from sales would not meet their debt requirements.

This practice had been very prevalent in areas of rapid growth such as Texas, Florida, and California, and S&L companies were faced with the fact that they had billions of dollars loaned on projects, and the value of the projects was less than the loans. The borrowers were not meeting their principal or interest payments, which led to the well-known S&L crisis. The crisis quickly developed into a national scandal, implicating a lot of developers and S&L officials who had fabricated or overstated the value of their projects.

Unfortunately, we were caught up in this crisis, even though we had borrowed responsibly. While we borrowed like other developers, we always maintained a 10 to 20% equity in the project. We needed the money not only to buy the land but to develop it - to put in roads, water and sewer, recreation facilities, and so forth. We had received the money to acquire the land and begin construction in a dozen or more large projects. We had the potential sales for the lots; however, the S&L companies that we were doing business with were caught up in this crisis and could not or would not fund their obligation to supply money to develop the lots. We found ourselves with a large debt of some $36 million, but with no ability to develop lots which would enable us to retire our debts.

The Savings and Loan scandal had become not only an economic disaster, but a political football, since the Federal Deposit Insurance Corporation (FDIC) was involved in insuring a lot of these Savings and Loan companies. A bill was passed by the United States Congress creating the Resolution Trust Agency. This agency took over the operation of all the bankrupt Savings and Loans corporations, including those that we were associated with. The RTA, working under pressure from Congress to clean up the mess as quickly as possible, began an incredible liquidation of properties in an already depressed market. What they could not recover, they demanded immediate repayment on. Of course, all of our loans were secured by real estate whose value had been greater than the loans, but depressed market conditions resulted in a $12-15 million shortfall in our re-payment.

I had the finances to cover the third of this debt for which I was responsible. The problem was that my partners had hidden their assets in such a way that it didn't appear as if they had the funds, though I knew they did because we had discussions about it. When development loans of the type we utilized were made, the borrowers would have to endorse, that is stand for, the loan or any deficiency. There was a phrase in the loan language called "joint and several" that allowed the RTA to come after a part-ner for repayment in part or for all of the debt, which is what happened to me. Realizing that elevating the situation into a fight or a legal battle with my partners would not resolve the issue, I negotiated, assuming their interest and obligations, and worked out a repayment schedule with the banks.

At the same time, a business associate of mine who was having financial difficulty was bothered by the fact that I had worked out a pay-out plan and was not living as if I was completely out of funds. This man tried to have the court force me into bank-ruptcy, and while the court action failed, it negated the pay-out plan I had secured with the banks be-cause of certain provisions in the RTA legislation.

I was astounded and upset over having to tell Dot. I had not kept the financial problems from her, but neither had I gone into detail, hoping that bank-ruptcy was preventable. I paid off a substantial part of my partners' obligations, but eventually exhausted all of my resources. I paid off every contractor or individual that was owed money, and the only outstanding obligation was this deficiency with the financial institutions. After I exhausted all my resources, I had only one of two options – either have liens filed, which I could not realistically ever satisfy or declare personal bankruptcy. My company, W. R. Henderson and Associates, honored all of its obligations, but since my wife and I were personally on the endorsements, we were personally responsible for the deficiency. Declaring personal bankruptcy was extremely distasteful, but after prayerful consideration and the advice of my attorneys and accountants, this seemed to be the only reasonable choice.

We proceeded to declare bankruptcy under chapter seven of the bankruptcy code. This process meant that we virtually lost everything we owned, including all personal property.

Dot and I prayed continually during this time for the strength to make it through. The most difficult moment came when we had to vacate our home with 24-hours notice. We did not have the money to hire a moving company. On the day that we had to move, a dozen or so friends from our church showed up with trucks and packed 45 years of accumulation into boxes and moved them and our furniture to a storage facility.

I mentioned that there were certain things I believed I could never endure, a sort of "Anything you ask of me God, just not . . ." sort of arrangement. The idea of a trailer home was right up there with what I felt I just could not, or should not, have to endure. When I told Dot about the bankruptcy, she quietly accepted it, as she had everything else. I remembered her words over again from when she had warned me that something wasn't right with the business partners from Florida. I remembered my foolish belief that somehow I could manage to keep an eye on it all.

As we stood together watching our friends pack up our home and wondering where God would lead us, I was amazed by the strength of my wife and the incredible blessing of our friends. Looking back, that day was one of the most joyful I have ever experienced because I felt such a richness in the people I was surrounded by. Through no effort of my own could I bear us up through this tragedy. I couldn't avoid the bankruptcy. I couldn't spare my wife what felt like a terrible embarrassment. But she didn't complain, and our friends made the whole affair seem like a strange celebration. I felt as if God were telling me, "Henderson, this is something you need to go through. None of the material possessions matter."

There was another lesson there as well. I had been charitable my whole life and had always believed there was little that separated those who found themselves in unfortunate situations and those in a position to give. If it weren't for the grace of God, any person might find themselves in need instead of being able to help. I truly believed this and was thankful for what we had. I tithed to the church and donated to charities out of a grateful heart that God had provided us with such abundance. But charity seemed easier when I was giving it, not receiving it. This was the first time I had been on the receiving end, the first time I had to look and ask for help. We had been poor when I was growing up, but we always had a decent home provided by the Methodist church and food on the table. I realized that it was as important to give with a grateful heart, as it was to be able to receive charity with kindness and grace because that was what God was offering. None of us deserved God's grace and salvation. I was prepared that day to live in a trailer if that was all we could find because there were people out there who didn't even have the friends we did to help us pack and move.

There was a time when I believed that God had been rewarding me for good behavior with business success. I had a need to please other people through success and achievements, and I realized how much financial independence meant to me. When a person has little, it is easy to be thankful for and appreciative of the little that's there. Success has a way of changing what one sees as the basic necessities of life, and I had happily walked down that path for over 45 years by the time we had to declare bankruptcy.

I smiled at Dot, thinking of our wedding vows, "for poor or for poor." We went from the year we started the laundry with my brother, barely able to rub two nickels together because of the loan, to now, losing our home. God was reminding me how difficult it is for a rich man to enter the kingdom of heaven because rich men rarely have their hearts and minds on the wealth of heaven.

While I was willing to live in a trailer if need be, God provided an alternative. It turned out that another friend of ours was spending the summer in Europe, and they offered us their home while they were gone. Fortunately, we were able in a few short months to continue our business and generate sufficient income to lease housing accommodations. Through friends and investment partners, we were able to slowly recover and satisfy any valid obligation that had not been satisfied.

"If you love me, you will obey what I command. And I will ask the Father, and he will give you another Counselor to be with you forever – the Spirit of truth. The world cannot accept him, because it neither sees him nor knows him. But you know him, for he lives with you and will be in you."   *John 14:15-17*

Chapter 22

Seeing the Light

I WAS WORKING IN THE GARDEN IN THE home we had built several years after the bankruptcy. We had managed after several months and help from friends to struggle back to our feet. God had blessed us richly since that time, and I continued to work in real estate development.

On this day, it was early but hot and humid already. While mulching around a tree, I suddenly felt light-headed and short of breath, cold but sweaty. Dot found me half-kneeling on the ground in obvious distress. I knew enough of the symptoms to realize it was a heart attack.

"Let me call Michael," Dot said. "Just stay right there," she said, and I could hear the shakiness in her voice. She ran into the house like I hadn't seen her move in a long while.

My body was feeling panicky but my mind felt calm. The ambulance arrived and carried me to the hospital. All the while, as the medical technicians worked to stabilize me during the ride, I felt such peace and a lightness in my soul that God was in control. It was like every joyful moment in my life was packed in tight around me.

"You were lucky," the doctor told me. "You got here in time."

I didn't feel luck had anything to do with it. It was as if anything left after the bankruptcy, any remaining sense of my self as deserving was stripped away at that point. It is as difficult to describe as combat because it was not as if God spoke out loud, or I saw some magical sign. There was this sense of safety and certainty that no matter what happened at that moment, God was in complete control.

There was a moment when my hospital room was quiet, relatively speaking, with the absence of family, visitors, nurses and doctors. The hum and beep of machines verified I was still alive, functioning properly. I surveyed my room, the flowers and cards, my drink cup with the straw, a book. I felt rested but restless. A noise near the door drew my attention.

"Well, you're new," I said to the nurse who entered my ICU room.

"Not new, just curious. I work down on the Peds floor. One of the nurses told me about a gentleman in ICU who was overjoyed after having a heart attack. I figured I had better get the story," she told me, walking up to my bed, checking monitors out of habit, before she returned her eyes to me.

"Overjoyed? I suppose I am," I replied.

I spent a good while telling her how God had worked in my life, how here at the end of it, He still cared enough to continue to deepen my faith. There were so many times in my life when death seemed more a certainty than not, yet here I was, for what?

"It was for this," I told her, "for this."

The Bible says in Psalms 71: 7-8: *"My life is an example to many, because you have been my strength and protection. That is why I can never stop praising you; I declare your glory all day long."* I had a new sense after the heart attack of what was unnecessary in my life – the country club member-ships, for example, suddenly seemed rather unim-portant – and what God was now calling me to do. I had held back small areas of my life from God's con-trol, but in order to be a full witness to his wonderful redeeming power, I had to be willing to trust every-thing to God.

Five years later, in the middle of a staff meeting, I realized I was having a stroke. One of my business associates looked frightened to death as we waited for the ambulance to arrive.

"Don't worry about it," I told him, as if we were talking about a small cut on my hand. Life and death at this point boiled down to death then life, and my soul was ready if God wanted to take me.

I suffered some loss of mobility on my left side, but otherwise the stroke did not affect my modest mental capabilities. Apparently the doctors discovered a skipped heartbeat, a condition which could have been present for some time. The skipped heartbeat had let through a blood clot, and the doctors assured me that I was fortunate because the stroke could have been much worse.

I could no longer garden the way I liked or move about as quickly as I wished. However, my mental faculties that God had been using for the last five years or so to be a better Christian example and to continue to make money for the causes we sponsored remained intact. I thought of the message in Ephesians 1:11: "It's in Christ that we find out who we are and what we are living for. Long before we first heard of Christ, . . .he had his eye on us, had designs on us for glorious living, part of the overall purpose he is working out in everything and everyone."

The unexamined life is not worth living. Socrates

I T TOOK BANKRUPTCY, A HEART ATTACK, and a stroke over the 80 years of my life to bring to completion a faith that had already been well-grounded in my youth. I'm convinced it took that long because somewhere along the way, I stopped seriously questioning the growth of my faith, if I ever seriously questioned it all. My impetus for writing this book, aside from my family, was for Christians and non-Christians to look at what I was able to accomplish in my life, only to realize at the end – the end of the book and for me near the end of my life – that none of it was possible without God having used me. Nobody would think twice about Michael Jordan scoring over 30 points in a basketball game; but if a freshman on some junior high school team scored the same amount of points, people would be amazed. That's what I'm talking about.When I reflect upon the life of a skinny, ordinary son of a poor Methodist minister, a boy who was pretty much of a nobody until he was out of his teens and then was blessed over his lifetime with awards and accomplishments, a man who suffered through bankruptcy, a heart attack and a stroke, I am amazed that life was mine. No one knows more than I do what a truly ordinary child I was.

Somewhere along the way, through those accomplishments, I failed to make a full commitment to living a life a faith – the kind of life that constantly questions and checks the level of dedication and trust. I believe God used the bankruptcy and the stroke and heart attack to show me where my faith level was. It is not enough to simply live a good life because living a good life can be deceptive. The awards and successes can lead a person to believe that he or she is in control of what is happening and is the source from which all these good things spring. But what happens when the wealth and success aren't there anymore – do we lose a sense of who we are or are we strong enough in the faith to know that what matters is God's love and sacrifice.

Too many people see faith as a shot in the arm or like a course of antibiotics that will make everything well. About a week into the two-week course of antibiotics, we start to forget to take the pill, and then we decide to throw the bottle away because, after all, we're feeling better. That's not faith. Faith is a day to day decision to live for Christ because he died for us – not just for the wealthy or the white-skinned or those who live in the right neighborhood and belong to a country club. None of those things matter because inside we are as sinful as the next man. When I stood on my porch the day had to vacate our house, I realized that if I used my wealth and success as the basis for how I defined myself, I would be nothing if I lost them because they are the things of the earth. If I turned to God and realized that all my blessings came from him, and that my purpose in life came through him, then nothing could happen to me that would destroy my sense of self-worth.

The church in America seems to have forgotten that we not only must believe in our minds, but in our hearts that Jesus is the son of God, and that such belief demands action. It takes a superabundant amount of faith and determination to live the life we have been created for – to recognize that we are bound by a commitment to live according to God's commandments and precepts. Failure is a certainty, but faith is about growth over one's lifetime. Success was a test. Bankruptcy was a test. Iwo Jima was a test. Where and to whom would I turn in each of those circumstances for faith and hope? Even more, where during the course of everyday would I turn for guidance and sustenance?

What God did for me, He can do for anyone no matter how dark a person's past has been or how empty the life. I heard about an experience at a forward medical evaluation and evacuation station in Iraq, though I cannot say it happened exactly this way. As the wounded solders were brought in, they were segregated: those who were wounded but would survive without immediate medical assistance were tagged with a white tag; those who were wounded but had a good chance of survival with immediate medical attention were tagged with a red tad to be evacuated ASAP; and those who were severely and mortally wounded with virtually no chance of survival were tagged with a blue tag. One of the attending nurses noticed that one of the solders with a blue tag had regained consciousness and appeared to be alert. She knelt down beside him and whispered in his ear. While he was wounded, he replied to her question. She asked his name, where he lived, what his family was like. As she questioned him, he appeared to get increasingly stronger. His whole body, which had been convulsing with pain, became still and the convulsions ceased. The nurse quietly removed the blue tag and replaced it with a red tag. As she ministered to him, his body relaxed and he gained strength. It was reported that he made a full and complete recovery.

No matter how despicable and miserable a person, no matter how dark the past, a life can be completely changed by the power of Jesus. Moving from a life of no hope to a life of hope, from a blue tag life to a red tag life, from a red tag life to a joyful white tag life.

Jesus said, "If you love me, you will keep my commandments." As important as believing in His commandments, His laws and precepts, it's more important that we be obedient to what we believe. For a long time after my commitment to Jesus, I lived the life of a want-to-be like Jesus, delaying making that total final surrender until certain goals, aspirations, and circumstances were achieved. I realized I was not being obedient, at which time I became a going-to-be, regardless of my goals, aspirations and circumstances, depending totally on Him. Someone told me a story, which may or may not be true, but the point is valid nonetheless. The story was about a young woman who became so discouraged and depressed she decided to commit suicide. She climbed up on a high bridge spanning the Mississippi river and was prepared to jump. A man who was fishing nearby looked up and saw what she was about to do, he ran up on the bridge in an effort to stop her but she jumped before he could reach her. As she fell into the water, without hesitation, he jumped in with the intent to save her and only then did he remember he could not swim. As he was thrashing around attempting to stay afloat, the woman noticed his situation and forgetting about herself she swam over and pulled him safely to shore. Reflecting on his experience he stated he was not saved by a person but saved by a purpose. Later they were happily married.

I am no accident – I was created for a purpose, but not a human purpose, a divine purpose. The purpose of my life was not my success and accumulation of wealth – it was how I could use that to accomplish God's goals. Over the last ten to fifteen years since the bankruptcy, stroke, and heart attack, I have come to this increasing realization. I needed to give up on the goals I had created for myself and to surrender them to what God's goals were for my life. I am no longer captive and imprisoned by the desire for approval of mankind.

Frankly, it's an awesome, fearful and exciting experience to really trust God to direct and control my life. I have discovered that for me to be able to see and hear His directions, I have to be in constant communications with Him, through prayer, meditation and the study of His word. As the song and Scriptures say, "It's no longer I that liveth, but Christ Jesus who liveth in me." I'm no longer responsible for the results, only to be available as an instrument to be used to bring about His desired results.

This is true freedom for me that has empowered and energized me to achieve some modest accomplishments. For this very ordinary man, I know that I never could have achieved what has been done by me and through me, except by divine motivation and empowerment. Why would God be willing to sacrifice His only Son so that an ordinary, sinful man like myself may enjoy fellowship with Him and receive abundant life, overcoming the world in this life and looking forward to spending eternity in a perfect, indescribable kingdom which we know as heaven, for eternity? To put it in human terms, not only is this the greatest life you can live, but it has an absolutely incomparable retirement plan. How wonderful it is to experience such love.

Finally, there's one confession I must make: It has been difficult for me to bypass my intellect. As the Scripture says, one must become as a child, completely trusting, completely believing that God will take care of you provided you live according to God's commandments. It is so good that our human intelligence has difficulty accommodating such a wonderful gift. The Scripture also says that God's ways are not our ways. How can we understand the infinite intelligence of God with our puny minds? This mystery becomes a reality as we fellowship with God and live according to His commandments. As a hard-nosed, bottom-line, Marine Corps combat Veteran who has experienced repeated attacks from the evil one, suggesting it's all a figment of man's imagination, and emotional need, I resoundly declare, it's real, it's real, and as the ad from a few years ago stated: Try it – You'll like it. I did, and I do. And so will you. God bless your exciting journey.

Epilogue